Contents

The Economy Has Left the Building

Rosa Kerosene

The economy's in an uproar,
the whole damn country's in the red.
Taxi fares are goin' up,
you say, "Billy Green is dead?"[1]

There's a level of abstraction in any discussion of 'markets' or 'economies' that is not only hard to avoid, it is paralysing. You probably wouldn't believe, for instance, the sweat and confusion that's gone into writing this short introduction. What you are reading now is the version in which I gave up, and just tried to say it the way I see it, even though I only see part of it. This journal, therefore, needs to be viewed as an attempt to confront this confusion and to clarify what needs to be done. It is trying to get to grips with a 'crisis' that was up and running well before the current credit crunch/perfect-storm/big freeze sequence; an ongoing financial meltdown that's had global ramifications, and has now caught up with the global middle class.

In trying to describe the situation here, it feels as if the description itself has entered, what John Barker refers to as, "the crisis of the integrity of information" (page 58). A general level of distrust and misinformation that, while most acutely felt in the financial sector, has burst into all other realms reliant on 'information'. The financial crisis, in its hegemonic formulation, is largely the realm of financial journalists and economic specialists. As a counterpoint, what this journal provides is a version of the events that relates the 'big freezes' and 'perfect storms' to the more personal and perhaps less abstract crises of soaring debt, variable interest rates, unemployment and bankruptcy. Or, as Massimo De Angelis has pointed out, to the techniques involved in binding people's fates directly to that of a failing, global, capitalist economy (page 7). This is a crisis, whose effects can be seen and felt in the workplace, in the home, and in the market-oriented restructuring of education.

The other major threads here concern the nature of the struggle against capital, and how in redefining 'work', one can better understand what, how and where this struggle takes place. Silvia Federici posits the crucial feminist analysis of women's unpaid reproductive labour as central to capitalist accumulation, as it involves the work of creating capital's most important commodity: labour power itself. In doing so, she opens up a whole field of struggle that takes place outside of the demonstration or strike, and engages with the creation of a "self-reproducing movement"(page 89). Tiziana Terranova and Marc Bousquet posit a similar role for the university by suggesting a radical rethinking of the role of the student, not as a customer in the "education supermarket", but as a form of hyper-exploited labour, opening up the student struggle to the general labour movement, as well as emphasising the role the university plays in reproducing capitalism, not only ideologically, but as a site of direct accumulation and exploitation as well(page 44). In his analysis of the relations between education and capitalism, Stewart Martin takes this a step further by positing the question of autonomy within the teacher-student, capital-labour relation (page 33). He calls for a struggle to "wrest non-capitalist life from capitalist life", echoing Federici's call for a struggle "against reproductive labour that would not destroy ourselves or our communities" and that collectively confronts capital "at every moment of our lives."

In order to investigate the various forms the fight against capital has recently taken, we've collected local accounts of repression and protest in a number of European cities. From direct challenges to the power of finance capital and private equity in London, an experimental living/squat action in Copenhagen, to tales of the intolerance and palpable vulnerability of neoliberal rule in Glasgow and St. Petersburg, we've laid out a small, and by no means comprehensive, cross-section of the challenges being posed to the dictates of neoliberal capitalism (page 75).

A key task of this journal is to introduce the market 'failure' of a capitalist economy – the repressive destructive nature of a system that works for the few at the expense of the many – into the comfortable discussions on how universities might best suit the interests of the labour market; or how everyone might best become a professional member of the creative middle class. This debate must be set against the economic and political reality of massive debt, price hikes, wage decreases, and the general squeeze on labour, within the context of what can only be described as capitalism's ongoing and permanent state of crisis.

[1] Gil Scott Heron, *Billy Green is Dead*, 1972

Next Lap in the Rat Race?
From Sub-Prime Crisis to the "Impasse" of Global Capital[1]

Massimo De Angelis

Why is it that fuel prices are increasing, home values are falling, credit is squeezed and job insecurity increasing? Why is it that more and more US working class families are suffering from the pinch of this crisis?

My answer might sound very cynical: It's so the system that links their working lives to those of billions of others around the world can continue, in new ways, to divide working people here and around the world; to devalue their work and reward those who bet on the "right" asset; pit one livelihood against another in a condition of endless competition; and thus reproduce scarcity in the midst of plenty. The many current crises that are hitting the world are interlinked, and what started in the US as a sub-prime and foreclosure crisis, is now appearing in other parts of the world as a food and energy crisis which is now, in turn, rebounding in the US. To put it bluntly, the current crises create the conditions for a planetary restructuring to allow the planetary rat race to continue, and continue producing scarcity in the midst of plenty. Unless, of course, people from around the world set limits on this madness, and restructure the way they produce the world's wealth together from below. Let us explore some of these linkages.

Financial crisis

The US is in the midst of two interrelated crises, an economic slowdown and a financial crisis. Recessions and slowdowns are means to devalue wages and put pressure on the working class and lay the basis for a profitable new upturn in the business cycle. This financial crisis has even deeper implications, because of its international ramifications, its links to other global crises such as food and energy, and the fact that faith in future growth, accumulation and repayment of past and current debt has been deeply shaken.

One of the top priorities of the US government and of other major players in the global economy, is to restore faith in the system and the promises it makes, because that faith keeps the system of capitalist

---

[1]Published in *UE News* in two parts, June and July 2008, United Electrical, Radio and Machine Workers of America, Pittsburgh, USA.

production going. However, the problem for the working class in the US, and across the world, is that this faith can be reestablished only to the extent the major players are convinced that a future of profitability and accumulation lies ahead. In other words, politicians will have to create the conditions of profitability *today* in order to give any hope of future profit to financial and industrial capitalists around the world. The current crisis, therefore, can be viewed as an opportunity for capital to restructure global capitalism and squeeze more out of workers and communities everywhere.

This crisis of global proportion became manifest in the US last summer, when the sub-prime crisis hit the headlines behind rising foreclosures and family bankruptcies. It followed a series of burst bubbles and Federal Reserve interventions on interest rates which kept inflating the economy with debt. In the late 1990s, the dot-com bubble burst and high tech stocks crashed, opening a recession. After the 9/11 attacks, there were widespread fears of financial collapse, as employment kept dropping throughout July 2003 (in spite of the recession being "officially over" in November 2001). Between January and December 2001, the Fed cuts its benchmark interest rate 11 times, dropping the key lending rate from 6.5 percent to 1.75 percent. This led to negative real interest rates (when inflation was factored in), which meant that banks borrowed money to make loans, and in real dollars, repaid less than they had borrowed. Cheap credit was a strategy to avoid and delay financial collapse and consequent global meltdown, but it is also how the Fed created the next bubble.

The Housing Bubble

After the dot-com crash, the era of easy credit led to speculation on the housing market. Home mortgage debt begun to show double digit growth, settling at around 16.6 percent a year in the period between 2000-2005, compared to about 9.2 percent a year in the 1990s. This added to other working class indebtedness (such as credit card debt), which grew through the last three decades. Loans were made available to working class people, who would not have qualified previously, because of low income or inadequate assets, and lenders did not seem interested in checking borrowers' statements. This was not only due to cheap credit, but also to the way mortgages were packaged into more complex debt instruments (which also led to the international ramifications of the crisis.)

The main difference between the traditional mortgage system and the new one that emerged with recent "financial innovations" in the US is the complicated web of linkages *away* from the mortgage-issuing banks.

In the "old days", mortgages were a simple affair between home buyers and banks. Banks had an incentive to minimize the risk of default, and to some degree, to renegotiate mortgage terms if there was a risk of default. The mortgage deal was confined in the relation between issuing bank and the borrower.

The novel aspect of the "new" mortgage market is the banks' offloading of risk to the market through *securitization*, i.e. the repackaging of these mortgages (home buyers' *promises* to pay back the loan with interest) into securities that combine a wide range of risks and promises of repayment by a variety of agents; investments that were sold off to hedge funds, pension funds, and back to commercial banks themselves.

What is interesting is the system of incentives for different agents in their efforts to maximize profit. First, mortgage lenders – or at least their agents – were interested in maximizing the number of mortgage deals, as they received a fee for each deal closed. Therefore, they weren't very careful about minimizing the risk of default. The rating agencies, such as Goldman Sachs, who were supposed to rate these mixed securities of bundled mortgages on a scale of risky to safe had an interest in overrating them. Why? Because rating agencies have competitors, and if they fail to please their clients with good ratings too often, these would turn to their competitors.

All these factors caused a drastic increase in home prices, which almost doubled in the 2000-2005 period (according to the Case-Shiller Home Price Index). Ultimately, however, this bubble burst. They always do, sooner or later. And the main, obvious reason is that debt must be paid back, with interest. And this is not always possible if the cost of repayment increases above what the borrower can afford. Thus, one factor contributing to the wave of defaults was the Fed's seventeen interest rate hikes between June 2004 and June 2006. The higher rates affected a variety of borrowers, but especially the more vulnerable ones with adjustable rate mortgages.

In July 2007, according to some estimates, a month before the official opening of the sub-prime crisis, home foreclosures were almost 100 percent above the previous year. The increase in foreclosures in turn contributed to a fall in further lending and a drop in home prices. By March 2008, average home prices measured by the Case-Shiller Index had fallen by almost 18 percent from their peak in June 2006. A fall in house prices in turn prevents many homeowners from playing the speculators' game (borrowing against the rising value of their houses) for the purpose of maintaining their livelihoods.

Livelihoods and speculation

The sub-prime story revealed some key changes in the way middle to low income US working class people secure a place to live. These changes are better understood if we consider them in the context of shrinking social entitlement to common wealth (which at the federal level is seen in the last three decades of tax cuts for the rich and social service cuts for the poor) and increasing "labor market flexibility" – job and wage insecurity – which increase the risk of default. The mandarins of finance have thought it out well: how to provide homes for the needy, while at the same time, reducing the investors' risk? The answer is the same as in every capitalist conundrum: turn "risk" into a commodity and pass it along.

The mortgage crash and the current crisis reveal that this "risk" was distributed to global markets, and appeared in investment portfolios ranging from American pension funds, to local governments in Europe, to international banks. According to some estimates, non-US investors hold about 60 percent of the mortgage-related debt that has defaulted or that it is likely to do so. There is a good chance that the mortgage on your home has been chopped up into small pieces and scattered around the world. The fact that nobody knows where "it" actually went, then caused banks to freeze their lending to each other, threatening to paralyze the international credit system and its huge need for *liquidity* (assets that can be easily bought and sold) to lubricate its daily operations.

This practice allowed increased exposure, but also increased expected profit. The push to sell mortgages was also met by eager home buyers who, in condition of declining real wages and the prospect of house price increases, saw the possibility to capitalize on a booming house market. For millions of workers, this meant their first opportunity to own their home; but the financiers also turned large sections of the working class into speculators, dividing them from workers with lower pay and no access to credit. Some workers supplemented declining wages by playing the markets, or by buying and "flipping" houses. In this way, their aspirations for social wealth in the form of health, education and housing were tied to the ups and down of financial markets.

Take, for example, the case of employers offering to partially pay workers in company stock, often as a bonus. The old "productivity deals" in the post-war period linked wage increases to absolute increases in productivity. But tying wages to the increases in share prices means tying them to *differentials* between these productivity increases and those of workers in competing companies. It makes the stock market the judge of whether workers are "sufficiently" productive, not in absolute terms, but relative to competitors, by rewarding (or not) the stock with an increase (or not) in its price. If competing firms use this technique to pay workers, the stock market decides which workers get wage increases. It is as if managers are saying to workers: Work harder, but how much you need to intensify your working life to get an increase in wages, neither you nor I will decide. The Market decides. And since nobody knows whether other workers in other companies will work more efficiently than you, uncertainty will push you to work even harder.

It must be clear that tying the conditions of reproduction (at both family and societal levels) to the ups and down of financial assets – whether these are shares of the employer's stock or the investment instruments that now drive housing prices – is to tie them to the dynamic of markets which fuel insecurity and further polarize wealth. This is an ingenious trick, because it undermines organized social struggle over wages and social entitlements like housing, health and education, in at least two ways:

    a) By making working class people in debt more vulnerable and therefore less willing to join in social struggles, since they're compelled to avoid default and the loss of future credit (increasingly the only source of higher living standards.)

    b) By pressuring them to work harder and accept worse conditions, which in turn stimulate cut-throat competitive struggle among workers.

Non-union workers heavily in debt are often too scared to join a union; union workers heavily in debt are more fearful of going on strike. The massive increase in all types of working class debt makes workers less able to resist the dictates of capital. The word *mortgage* derives from Latin, meaning "the grip of death." It evokes a condition in which a debtor loses freedom over their own lives, precisely because to reproduce their livelihoods they are compelled to get more cash to repay debt (which in standard economic language translates into "forcing cash flows.")

End of the neoliberal era?

The recent sub-prime crisis and its international ramifications could well indicate the end of the neoliberal era as we know it since it emerged in the late 1970s. *Neoliberalism* arose as a response by US capital to a threefold problem resulting from planetary struggles of the previous two decades:
    1) How to cut the social wage (wages plus social benefits) received by the US working class, but at the same time
    2) Allow in some way the reproduction of the US working class and
    3) Intensify their working lives (make people work harder).
The recent sub-prime experiment was the last of many attempts to deal

with this threefold problem. It must be understood within the framework of neoliberal changes and of the processes of global restructuring which followed them. (The term "neoliberalism" means a return to the "free market" ideology from the "Gilded Age" of capitalist robber barons, not some new era of generosity.) To understand the possible implications of this crisis, we must therefore, briefly trace the development of the conditions that made it possible.

1979 is the year in which Paul Volker – then chairman of the Federal Reserve – "officially" launched the neoliberal era with a sudden 1 percent increase in the interest rate, precipitating a global recession. The latter, in turn, created the conditions for neoliberal reforms, such as financial market deregulation, union busting, cuts in social entitlements, tax cuts for the rich, and intensified free trade. The massive explosion in debt and financial markets (of which the subprime crisis is the latest expression) were a major consequence of this. "Excessive" public spending was identified as the major source of inflation and unemployment, together with "excessive" wage demands. With the election of Margaret Thatcher in the United Kingdom in 1979, and Ronald Reagan in the US in 1981, a new "consensus" started to consolidate among world rulers according to whom national assets had to be privatized for, public spending curbed, and capital markets had to be liberalized. Until then, the post-World War II governments could implement Keynesian policies of full employment – whether these were successful or not – through the manipulation of tools such as the interest rate, the exchange rate, taxes and government spending (Keynesian policies, based in the economic theories of John Maynard Keynes, began to be applied by governments during the 1930s, and became orthodoxy across the West after WWII.)

With the opening up of capital's markets, governments decreed the abandonment of their commitments to full employment and any form of the welfare state or social safety net. Economic and social policies must please the financial capital markets. If governments granted popular concessions that redistributed resources from capital to the working class, financial capital would fly away, thus inducing a fall in exchange rates and an increase in interest rates and provoking a downturn in business and an increase in unemployment. In the view of neoliberals, a "stable economy" meant accommodation to the desires of international financial capital. Financial markets thus started to exert heavy pressure on conditions of work – whether waged work in factories or offices or unwaged work of raising children and reproducing lives in the home – through capital's increased ability to migrate from place to place, pitting conditions of working class reproduction against one another. Governments now competed against one another to cut the public spending that was part of the social wage: education, health, housing, to mention just a few.

In the global South, which did not have "advanced" capital markets through which to impose the discipline of global capital, the same effects were obtained through the management of what became known as the *Third World debt crisis*, precipitated by Chairman Volker's interest rate increase. In the event of a liquidity crisis in a debtor country, the first response is a phone call to the International Monetary Fund (IMF) in Washington. The response to such a phone call by a national government is well known: IMF officials offer their help and will consider extending a loan in order so the country in question meets its debt payments to the big global bankers. This would allow it to continue to "benefit" from existing trade agreements, aid flows, and all the perks that go with being a member of the world "economic community."

However, the proviso for the loan would be a series of conditions, also known as a Structural Adjustment Program (SAP), which the IMF forced all countries in crisis to adopt with little variation: devalue the currency, thus making imports more expensive and enforcing a cut in real wages; privatize water, education, healthcare and other national resources, thus opening them up to restructuring, hence unemployment; cut social spending; cut subsidies on necessities like food and fuel; open up markets to foreign investors; promote competitive exports, which will help to repay the debt. In the case of basic resources like water, their privatization results in attempts to make poor people pay for them at prices they often cannot afford. Millions of people across the world have struggled against these enclosures (dispossession or privatization of resources essential to subsistence), thus slowing them down, sometimes even stopping them for the time being.

But as in the case of financial liberalization in the global North, the management of debt crises became an opportunity to enclose common resources, and make people more dependent on the markets in the South, too. In both the North and the South, through financial deregulation and free trade, neoliberal capital thus aimed to turn the "class war" of the 1960s and 1970s – when capital's power faced challenges in communities, factories, offices, streets and fields around the world – into a planetary "civil war". A civil war fought through competition, a way of life that pits each community of workers against every other.

It has done this by mechanisms of competition that have come to pervade every sphere of life. It has done this by demands for "efficiency" – lowering the costs of production – which in fact means *shifting* its costs away from capitalists and onto the environment, communities, and human bodies (where they don't count as economic costs). It has done it through the management of borders with detention camps, deportation, and the criminalization of migration by xenophobic and racist laws and practices.

In this context, the development of information and communication technologies, together with the drastic reduction in the monetized (but not the environmental) cost of global transport, has offered capital a major opportunity to restructure global production and construct a system that facililates its escape from zones of organized working class strength.

Through the late 1970s and 1980s, *export processing zones* (EPZ's) began to mushroom around the world. These are areas set up by governments in the global South, in which extremely favorable tax regimes for business, slack environmental regulations, and anti-union laws, in a context of widespread poverty and increased dependence on the market, all help industries that want to escape the higher wages and stronger regulations of the Northern countries. The *maquiladora* zone along the US-Mexican border is the best-known example in North America. With the generalization of EPZ's to whole countries (such as Mexico since NAFTA), *multinational corporations* increasingly turned into *transnational corporations*. While the former, which grew in the 1950s and 1960s, replicated production processes in different countries so as to access national and regional markets, the latter slices up the production that once took place in one area, and displaces it through large *global production networks* according to cost and efficiency criteria. The productive nodes within these networks might belong to a major transnational corporation, or they might be subcontracted to minor players.

Devaluing and dividing workers

This global restructuring developed in the last few decades, along with the development of financial speculation and the use of debt, has allowed the reduction in the value that the mental, physical, and affective capacities of US workers have *for* capital. This value, which we call the *value of labor power*, does not directly correspond to the wage received by workers, although it is linked to it. It also depends on the prices of the goods and services that are typically consumed by workers, and the latter depend both on their condition of production and the general level of inflation.

The global restructuring made possible by the enclosure of resources and entitlements created the conditions for widening the wage hierarchies (both global and local) – the latter reproduced culturally through xenophobia and racism, and economically, through pervasive competition and forced dispossession. These wage gaps, in turn, made it possible to reduce the value of labor power in countries like the US without a proportional decline in living standards, by lowering the price of commodities that enter in the wage basket of these workers. So, for example, the planetary expansion of sweatshops in global commodity chains means that US workers can buy pants or digital radios at Wal-Mart at low prices. Because of cheap service labor from the South and East – the result of massive poverty caused by Structural Adjustment – many Americans now hire Philipina or Mexican women to take care of their children and aged grandparents.

Meanwhile, in the South, this process has made it possible to discipline new masses of workers into factories and assembly lines, fields, and offices, thus enormously extending capital's reach in defining the terms – the what, the how, the how much – of social production.

In both the North and the South, the enclosure of resources that formerly belonged to all in common, means an increased dependence of the working class on markets to reproduce livelihoods, less power to resist the violence and arrogance of those whose priority is only to seek profit, less power to prevent the market from running their lives. It makes working class people more prone to fratricidal wars against other workers who are trapped in the same competitive race, but with different levels of rights and different access to wages. All this has meant a generalized state of *precarity*, where life is precarious and nothing can be taken for granted.

Global circuits

From the point of view of global finance, what allows the *dynamics* described above is what generally is described as Bretton Woods II and which is expressed by the enormous US trade deficit and correspondent surplus in China and other exporting countries. It is the interlink between surplus and deficit countries that allows them to generate eternally new debt instruments like the one that has recently resulted in the sub-prime crisis. The ongoing recycling of accumulated surplus of countries exporting to the US, such as China and oil producing countries, is what has allowed financiers to create new credit instruments in the US.

Hence, the "deal" offered by the elites in the United States to its working people has been this: 'you give us a relative social peace and accept capitalist markets as the main means through which you reproduce your own livelihoods, and we will give you access to cheaper the consumption of goods, access to credit, and the illusion that gains in terms education, health, pensions, and social security could be made through the speculative means of stock markets and housing prices.'

In turn, to allow the reproduction of the labor power of 250 million unemployed, under-employed and dispossessed Chinese, the "communist" leaders need double-digit rates of growth, and therefore, they need both Western markets and their capital, know-how and technologies. It is for this reason that they have been willing to recycle their enormous trade surpluses back to the US, thus contributing to the liquidity for the expansion of the many forms of debt in the US. This is a vicious cycle that locks everybody into an endless rat race.

At the same time, in China and other developing zones in the global South, people are being offered a different sort of deal: industrial employment at wages that, while very low by international standards, are still substantially higher than anything obtainable in the impoverished countryside. But there is also the promise attached to this that, through their link to global markets, their conditions of living will gradually be improved. While wages in many such areas seem to have been growing over the last few years, thanks to the intensification of popular struggles (particularly in China), such gains are impossible to generalize. What's being offered to the South is the promise to expand the existing urban middle classes, who already model their lifestyle and consumption patterns on Northern ones. Although an understandable longing for "betterment" is at the basis of what has been sold as the "American dream", what makes it a dream is precisely the fact that, even in the US, it has never meant eliminating wage hierarchies, just reshaping them. This is a game in which there must, necessarily, be losers.

At the global level, this is impossible to generalize for two reasons. First, no matter how much we recycle or how many energy efficient light bulbs we use, it would still require several planets to accommodate an "American dream" way of life modelled on high energy and individualized consumption patterns for six billion people. Secondly, precisely because this way of life requires the further expansion of competition of all against all, of borders and property regimes, of enclosures and dispossession, it must always necessarily be dependent on hierarchy and exclusion. In other words, middle class "betterment" is an illusion constructed in between the Scylla of ecological disaster and the Charybdis of poverty. The only thing that this model of development can create is gated communities of whatever is left of middle class families accessing privatized social services within the borders of their patrolled walls, surrounded by hordes of poor with little access to public services and whose entrance through the gates of those enclaves is managed for the purpose of serving those communities.

Many crises: what restructuring lies ahead?

The turn of the millennium saw a vast and sudden flowering of planetary popular uprising against neoliberalism in Latin and Central America, Africa, Asia and ultimately, within the cities of the former colonial powers themselves, and in the US. The global uprising occurred at the end of the Cold War era, when the massive global security apparatus was beginning to look like it lacked a reason of being, when the world threatened to return to a state of peace and claims were made for a "peace dividend" to be channeled into social entitlements.

The immediate reaction to this wave of struggles was a textbook case, helped by US former allies Al Queyda. The response was further tax cuts for capital and a return to global warfare with the funding of the 1 trillion dollar war in Iraq. However, this attempt to use US military power as the ultimate enforcer of the neoliberal model failed in the face of almost universal popular resistance as well.

Now, the very financial architecture that tied together the global circuits of capitalist production is in deep crisis. As a result, the neoliberal project lies shattered.

This is the nature of the current neoliberal "impasse": how to further the reach of production for profit globally in the face of global growing resistance to enclosures and dispossession, and in the wake of military and financial strategies that have reached their limit?

Therefore, the fundamental questions for capital today seem these: how to use the economic financial crisis triggered by the sub-prime crisis to push for new forms of governance and global restructuring aimed at promoting a new cycle of planetary accumulation? How can this restructuring be shown to address those strategic questions that are posed by growing social conflict worldwide, such as the question of energy, poverty, and environment?

In this, the elites might be helped by the emergence of new crises that are directly linked to the sub-prime one: the food and oil price hikes, which are devastating communities' livelihoods across the world, and are at the basis of current massive waves of struggles. Both oil and food prices have been rising as a combination of "fundamental" and "speculative" factors. Oil demand has been surging from the need posed by the growth in industrial production in many countries of the South described before against the background of a relatively sticky oil supply. Food prices in turn have been rising as a result of the expansion of agri-industrial models of land use, the concern of which is to feed global market demand (that is *paying* demand) not hungry people around the world. In recent years, land use has shifted first into animal feed production (due to the increase in meat consumption brought about by rapid urbanization in the South, but also in the North), and more recently, to biofuel, as oil prices make it profitable to use land for this purpose. On the speculation side, just as the bursting of the stock market bubble in the late 1990s shifted speculation into housing, so as now the burst in the housing bubble and stalling of world stock markets triggered by the sub-prime crisis, has shifted the interest of speculators away from these assets and onto commodities, which in turn fuel the price increase and create the condition for a new wave of global restructuring by the creation of massive poverty, both in the North and in the South.

They will try to use this crisis to attempt to reverse the gains of past social movements: to deal with the energy crisis and global warming, they will put nuclear energy back on the table, they will further commodify "guilt" by extending the reach of carbon trading, and they will focus on capital intensive alternative energy sources, in such a way as to ensure that whatever energy resources do become important in this millennium, it will be difficult to democratize them. To deal with the food crisis they will try to further the role of biotechnology and genetically modified foods that further impoverish poor world farmers and reduce food security. The World Bank is already suggesting that Sovereign Wealth Funds puts aside a small proportion of their money for food aid, but only as tied to a larger project of global restructuring.

They will also try to reshape the configuration of global production networks. A new class deal in China, for example, could be thought to go in this direction. From the perspective of global capital, the increasingly rioting workers in China could be allowed higher standards of living if new low wage zones are created elsewhere to help maintain a low value of labour power in the US and in Europe. In certain regions of Africa, for example, the continent where struggles defending common access to land, water, and social entitlements have been most intense in current decades, and where enclosures of these commons, in cases in which they succeeded, have left trails of social, community, and ecological devastation.

There are forces at work to create the global infrastructures necessary for this reconfiguration of global production and wage hierarchy. For example, the World Bank – deprived of its role of funding controversial dams and pipe-line projects across the world by the many poors' struggles, whose livelihoods were threatened by those projects – has been funding development in China's poorer provinces. In turn, this allows the Chinese government to carry out similar projects in Southeast Asia, Africa, and even Latin America, and to bypass the international mobilization that coagulated against the mega-projects funded by the World Bank.

Finally, the collapse of the value of the dollar, if maintained and managed, will further reduce the value of labor power of the US working class, cutting their access to goods and services. This will open the possibility of a partial reversal of foreign investment into manufacturing in the US, and the growth of outsourcing of global production networks back into the US, as it is discussed in some financial blogs. This job creation will of course depend on conditions of further impoverishment of already large sections of the US working class: the American dream turned nightmare.

It goes without saying that it will be up to the waged and unwaged working class everywhere to push back what really lies behind the promises of development and prosperity: further enclosures of entitlements and commons, a way of life dominated by the race to out-compete others, and therefore destined to reproduce wage hierarchies, exclusions, poverty, ecological disaster, and scarcity in the midst of plenty. The reclaiming of commons for our own times – as demonstrated by so many struggles around the world – is the minimum condition for reverting precariousness in the condition of work and living. But it is also the condition upon which new forms of local and trans-local communities of producers can be constituted, communities who reproduce livelihoods, while setting their own measures and value of things, without submitting to the measures and value of things imposed upon them by disciplinary capitalist markets or authoritarian hierarchies.

Intensities of Labour:
from Amphetamine to Cocaine

John Barker

1 The Miracle of Speed

At the end of the 1960s, young and cocky Situationists like myself talked of the Japanese economic miracle – because then it was the Japanese miracle – as being fuelled by amphetamine. The evidence was anecdotal, but it was well known that the cheaply-made drug was a major business for the Yakuza. This particular miracle was manufacturing-based; electronics and autos figured prominently. In modern parlance, it was Fordist, that is, large-scale manufacturing dependent on the 'mass-worker'. Amphetamine, known to us then as an all-night dancing drug, was perfect for long hours of work, while staying alert. As we saw it, the miracle depended on disposable workers subject to early burn out. A modern version of Marx's picture of capital and labour as the vampire and its victims.

Since then, in the richest parts of the world, the decline in the relative size of the manufacturing sector is common knowledge. At the same time, the shift to a services-based economy has involved what Maurizio Lazzarato has called an anthropo-sociological shift in the organisation of labour, prompting the concept of 'immaterial' labour. In addition, the generic term post-Fordist has come to be used as an umbrella description of these changes. They are real enough, but to see them as forming a discontinuity with what went before is too slick in manipulating theoretical categories, and leapfrogging the realities of global work.

The most common global economic model now is the super-exploitation of pre-Fordist sweatshops and a peasantry pressured from all sides. Fordism, where it does exist, is far from played out, though more often today it lacks the associated Keynesian virtue of the producing labour being able to buy what it produces, and so sustain 'effective demand'. In the rich world, too, sites of 'primitive accumulation' co-exist with Fordist and post-Fordist labour. As a new form of the organisation of labour, as Lazzarato recognises at an abstract level, post-Fordism itself began in the manufacturing sector. As more subdued Situationists in the 1970s, we talked of the model of team systems in Swedish car plants as self-exploitation. Since then in the rich world the global rhythm of just-in-time production, dependent on computerisation, has created new forms of rational exploitation. At the same time, the service sector has been subjected to the de-skilling and time-and-motion disciplines of industrial Taylorism. The language of factory discipline has been incorporated even into public services like education and health, which are full of 'line managers', while a more Stalinist-type of Taylorism has lead to the constant application of goals and targets to be reached.

What remains the common factor globally, is capital's compulsion to accumulate. For individual capitals, one has only to read the financial pages of most newspapers to see that the health, or otherwise, of companies is seen through this lens. Since the start of the general capitalist offensive in the mid 1970s, the pressure has been on wages, intensity of labour and the length of the working day, while it has made its own compulsion into a natural state of affairs. Much of this pressure is disguised by the mechanisms of the equalisation of rates of profit to make an average rate, whereby surplus value produced by labour-intensive sectors of production are realised by other 'capital-intensive' ones. But these pressures, despite enormous differences in real wages, are also global, with a universal push for a greater intensity of labour, though taking very different forms.

For example, take the privileged sector of immaterial labour as defined by Lazzarato: 'audiovisual production, advertising, fashion, the production of software, photography, cultural activities, etc' ... activities which tend to define and fix cultural artistic norms, fashions, tastes, consumer standards, and more strategically, public opinion.' Descriptions of this work in the 'immaterial labour' canon, however, do not look at the intensities of labour involved. The widespread use of cocaine in this sector is not accidental. Its availability in the UK obviously has to do with a range of factors – the nature of some Latin American economies and their staggering inequalities, sophisticated criminal organisation, the increasing rise in the worldwide transportation of material goods and so on – but it is also because the demand is there. It has been the perfect drug for this relatively privileged sector; not creative in any real sense, but perfect for generating an indiscriminate intensity of enthusiasm for the projects provided in this sector, and for believing in the great importance of what one is doing at any given time.

2 Pre-digital intensities

Just out of prison in the early 1990s, and in urgent need of finding a way back into the world and some legitimate income, preferably PAYE, [G]
I was lucky to get a job in the small world of overnight news clippings provision with no CV required. At that time, the business was pre-digital, and there is still a niche market for Chief Executives and the like who want their clippings neatly cut and pasted onto headed paper, or hard copy photocopies at least. The photocopy machines were the crucial

items of equipment (as they are for National Health Service line managers churning out new targets and organisational charts), and apart from a hard-working fax machine, they were the only 'fixed' capital in the place. Otherwise, it was more than just pre-digital. The building in Tooley Street – old, old London – was mass-produced gothic. The two floors occupied by the agency were covered in stained beige carpeting that turned up at the edges to show the nibbled grey foam underneath. The system demanded not just the photocopy machines, but wall-to-wall pigeon holes. Pigeon holes! Even then they were antique.

Each pigeon hole belonged to individual or collective clients, the odd one that was interesting, but mostly corporate bastards and financial PR bastards with their own client list. Most cuttings would go to more than one pigeonhole, ten or more were possible. Hence, the importance of the photocopier. Anywhere between two and four in the morning there could be sharp confrontations about access rights to the two, or sometimes three, machines on the go. And then it might be luck if the bastard you'd got hold of didn't jam somewhere down the line. Sometimes, it would clap out altogether, and we'd be down to two or just one machine for the night. Things would then get ultra-manic. Other times, with luck or skill, down on your knees, heart palpitating, you'd sort it yourself, easing the mashed up A4 out of a roller or gripper without leaving any paper scraps behind.

The only guides to help with this extra job were inadequate diagrams stamped somewhere on the copiers' surfaces. They may well have been stamped on by someone like Zhang Guo Hua, a Chinese worker who had entered the UK illegally and died after doing a 24-hour shift doing a similar stamping job. We instead, the Readers, were mostly odd balls, ex-art students, and long-term ex-students still paying off debts, and me, getting a foothold back in the 'real world': eclectic, déclassé 'middle class'. The job involved reading a morning paper, or two or three, first editions arriving between 10:30pm and 11pm, and cutting out any article of any interest to any client, and noting the other clients who would be interested in the same piece: the client/subject list ran to many pages. You might get say *The Independent*, *The Mail*, and *The Star*. Or if it was the *Financial Times*, it might just be *The Express* in addition. Or just *The Mirror*. Whatever, the job required sticking the correct tab, date plus name of paper, onto each cutting, and then dividing them into two piles. Some were to be mounted on various types of A4 as originals for big cheese clients with that kind of fetish; the others to be photocopied on reusable A4 in order that shadow did not appear.

In addition to us oddball 'middle class', there were some oddball 'proletarians', pals of one of two bosses, who did clipping mounting at this stage of the procedure, so that as a reader, one could get to the photocopier with both mounted and unmounted clippings. After that first bout at the machines, things got really crazy. You'd read, photocopied, distributed the mass of stuff into umpteen pigeon holes and then geared up for another fight for photocopier access. From reading plus first stage filtering, the new 'collectively' shared out responsibility was to prepare the packages for the clients. Various bastards at Barclays Bank or Price Waterhouse would like their clippings filtered into sections of interest so that at 6:30 a.m. they were ready for anything; at worst a routine grilling if the news was bad.

Our targets, deadlines, were never met in a wholly relaxed manner. Around 5:30 a.m. the drivers, cabbies and independents, impatient for the packages they were to deliver, were hovering. Other nights, as the dawn appeared over the river Thames, things got seriously manic. Lou the Taxi driver would be on my earhole to forget everything else and finish the Food and Drink Federation Package first so that he could get away. Other times, we'd be dragged into other packages, a Financial PR company wanting photocopy only, but mounted on its headed paper. All this so that some corporate bastard didn't have to read the paper himself. All this with the additional pressure that a 'miss' might mean the end of a contract. A spectacular hit on the other hand, a corporate name mention in a murder mystery story say, would get at most a 'good spot' mention. There were several nights after a bad-sleep day, random car alarms wanting to have their say, I would take a lick of amphetamine powder myself.

3 More productivity, more hard work

This was underpaid intensity of labour, which Marx describes plainly enough as 'expenditure of labour in a given time' in *Capital*. (Volume I, Chapters 17 and 21). Increased intensity, and the length of the working day, are contrasted with what he calls the 'productiveness' of labour as means of increasing the production of similar units by each worker. It is a contrast, because increases caused by the 'productiveness' of labour through the use of improved machinery which has involved a fixed capital outlay, and which he calls 'productive forces', do not increase the value or surplus value of the aggregate units produced, whereas increases in intensity and length of the working day do. This contrast becomes important in Volume III, Chapter 14, in which Marx outlines countervailing phenomena to what he calls The Tendency of the Rate of Profit to Fall – a tendency caused precisely by the increased weight placed on 'productiveness' in the production mix.

Such distinctions ought to be helpful in deconstructing the notion of 'productivity'. In the 1960s and 1970s explicitly named productivity deals were prevalent, and the notion of productivity continues to lurk in nearly all capital-labour negotiations to the degree that there are still such negotiations. There is, however, a problem with this Marxist deconstruction, in that ambiguity hangs over the relationship between intensity and productiveness as Marx describes it. He talks of the relative number of spindles as against the number of people employed in an international comparison: at one end France with one person per 14 spindles, and Britain with one per 78. But this does not tell us about the nature of the spindles. Are the British ones so technically superior that minding 78 does not involve a greater 'expenditure of labour in a given time' than minding 12? More specifically, does technically superior necessarily mean less work per machine? The text here (Volume I, Chapter 22) is not so helpful either: 'In proportion as capitalist production is developed in a country, in the same proportion do the national intensity and productivity there rise above the international labour.'

The notion of the intensity of labour, however, as well as length of the working day, is a valid one absolutely relevant to the present day capitalist offensive with its compulsion to accumulate and the associated aim of social control. Often, and in the Fordist model openly, there have been increases in what might be called 'pure' intensity of labour. What they called speed-up. For a long period, this was the area of labour-capital conflict in the car industry. As a measure of intensity, it was said that to work 'on the line' at Ford itself, 15 years was the maximum possible. What has been hidden is the extent to which the development of new types of machinery to increase the productiveness of labour has been dedicated to demanding a greater intensity of labour from those operating it rather than, as we might say, the machine taking the strain. A clear example is in the modern world of the logistics of global just-in-time production. Dockers are not just seeing the return of casual labour, but as Brian Ashton has pointed out, 'are subjected to work speeds that are set by automated guided vehicles (AGV's), automated stackers and semi-automated cranes.'

In the 1960s and 1970s, there was a recognition (both intellectually and in practice) that, despite the illusions on offer of more and more leisure time for the worker and what was he/she is going to do with it, machinery, developed under capitalism, never had taking the strain as its objective. In the early 1960s, in the powerful writing for the first issues of *Quaderni Rossi* (at the very beginning of the Italian autonomist movement), Raniero Panzieri used Marx's class analysis to override the notion of 'productive forces' being somehow neutral, let alone reaching the point of making capitalist relations of production untenable. Instead he argued, 'the relations of production are within the productive forces'; that technical development 'presents itself as a development of capitalism... as an exhibition of the capitalist's authority... and with new possibilities for the consolidation of its power.'

'Fordism', if looked at as productive processes, was and is shot through with 'Taylorism', with the time and motion study as its analytical tool. Harry Braverman, in *Labour and Monopoly Capital*, quite rightly saw both as being aimed at the de-skilling of labour and a consequent reduction of its economic and political power. In the car industry of the 1970s, this was aimed at the de-skilling of draughtsmen and factory engineers as punch hole NC's (Numerical Computers which pre-set lathes and milling machines) were introduced on the factory floor. At the same time, they increased surveillance and control of jobs done on the line. This had a double-impact on worker organisation. It radicalised draughtsmen and engineers in the newly formed TASS trade union. The most radical inside that union most famously formed the alternative plan for Lucas Aerospace in which machinery for arms production could be re-jigged into making socially useful products, in particular for the disabled. In the case of Ford itself, 'on the line' workers created an international organisation autonomous from the official trade union set-up. The Ford Workers Combine was capable of coordinating solidarity actions internationally at the shop steward level. Its imaginative tactics had a precision formed from a clear understanding of the productive process and changes in it.

More generally, at this time, increases in intensity of labour were met with go-slows, or fights over tea breaks. These latter were subject to much soggy bourgeois satire: tea breaks, Ho Ho Ho. More often this conflict was fought out in the arena of wages. This tended to disappoint various leftists talking about 'economism' in true Leninist fashion, but the level of sophisticated militancy was enough to provoke a systematic targeting of the pound sterling, as well as the Italian lira, by the new wave ideological US Treasury team of the Ford Administration lead by William Simon. They made explicit speeches to 'the market' to the effect that the lira and the pound were automatically transformed into Mickey Mouse currencies by the effects of labour militancy. In the new era of 'floating' exchange rates brought into being by Nixon's 1971 decision to break the link between the US dollar and gold (spelling the end of the Bretton Woods consensus), currencies could be targeted in this manner by words in the right ears from the representatives of a dollar massively strengthened by US control of OPEC's new wealth in the form of the petrodollar. This offensive scared the life out of the trade union leadership in both countries. Nevertheless, until the capitalist offensive that had been kicked off in this manner was augmented by a new era of de-skilling, and anti-union legislation, resistance to increases in intensity of labour continued.

4 New drudgery

Machinery, the very word has an old-fashioned ring to it, is too heavy for economies that are 'light' and 'flexible'. In the mid 1990s, when I first dipped my toe into what might loosely be called the digital economy, 'kit' was the favoured word. This dipping the toe involved a part-time removals business (me and my nephew in a clapped-out Luton van) specialising in creative digital office moves – into Soho or out, then into Clerkenwell or out – and some months back in the news clippings business, but this time working the first months of an online service. This required a different intensity of labour to the hard-copy clippings job. The reading of the papers remained the same, as was the size of the reading list, the number of papers per person rather higher, but there was none of that battling with the photocopier or the walks around the pigeon holes with armfuls of A4. Instead, a template existed on screen where, with the Tab key, you could set up the date and name of the newspaper; then a box for the headline of selected articles; then another box in which to give a one or two sentence summary of what it said; and finally a box in which to key in the codes for all the clients who might, or should, be interested in the relevant article.

Whether any of this work could be said to have created surplus value is dubious, it was by and large an aid to financial PR which creams off a margin of surplus value it has not itself created. Spin, they call it these days. The work, however, was profitable, and the company grew even before I left. As an individual I found its intensity less onerous, though night-shift work is bad for your health whatever the job, the evidence is legion. What it shared with the hard-copy business was its dependence on loyalty to fellow workers. Team loyalty, or in our case, shift loyalty was factored into the accounts, consciously or not, by the employers. This is hardly special, they say it is how armies work, how even the mass suicides of World War I continued month after month. Don't let your mates down. In the hard-copy job it was absurd, people tottering into work with the flu, and giving it to the rest of us, simply because they knew that the night's mania would be that much the greater without them. A related similarity was knowing that too many 'misses' would lose contracts, and that lost contracts would mean job losses.

With the online work there were, however, more ways of avoiding the intensity of labour which the process (writing two-line summaries of relevant articles) seemed to demand. Very soon, I had developed a set of bland summary templates. Underpaid and intensive as it was, though, it bore no relation to the conditions of work in data-processing shitwork in a Jamaican Export Processing Zone. RSI [G] is a reality, ask anyone who has ever suffered, or see how much corporate money has gone into legally proving that it does not exist. Export Processing Zones, almost by definition, rule out health and safety considerations or regulations.

5 The long day closes in

More recently, it is another of Marx's 'countervailing' phenomena, the length of the working day that has attracted most attention. It has come from four directions: socio-psychological concerns about 'work giving meaning to people's lives'; heroic accounts of how very rich people, such as those working for the McKinsey consulting firm or investment banks, work very long hours; grasping the material realities of new forms of exploitation – perverted forms like being on call all the time, but only being paid for the hours that you work, which is the cruelest manifestation of just-in-time; and Trade Unions now addressing the matter of overtime. Small attention has also been given to cases like Zhang Guo Hua in Cleveland, UK, mentioned above, and in China itself of He Chun-Mei, a 30 year-old woman, both of whom died after working 24-hour shifts. Such realities can provoke only grim mirth at slobbering accounts of investment bankers working 15-hour days in the Business and now the Feature pages of newspapers. Working 15 hours a day to make sure they get their cut of the 24-hour days of super-exploitation.

In the UK, this emphasis on the length of the working day is hardly surprising, given the long-drawn-out resistance to the European Union's 48-hour working directive from the New Labour government and its supposedly 'Old Labour' Chancellor. Figures from Prof Carey Cooper of Lancaster University showed that:

- the UK has the longest working hours in the Western World after the USA, having now surpassed those of Japan.
- in the last seven years, coinciding with the reign of New Labour, there has been a significant rise in employees working in excess of 48 hours; from 10% in the late 1990s to 26% in 2005.
- since 1992, there has been a leap of 50% in the number of women expected to do a 48-hour week.
- estimates in the 2000-2 period suggest that those doing a 60-hour week has increased by one third to approximately 17% of the total workforce.

Professor Cooper's inquiry determined that if a person worked consistently long hours it would damage their psychological and physical health. Once again, we are talking 'burn-out', and it is here that length of the working day and the intensity of labour (those sure-fire ways of extracting more surplus value), are likely to have the same effect. Taken in combination, as in the cases of Hu Chen-Mei and Zhang Guo Hua, they are likely to be fatal.

That they may be combined at all, reflects the defeats of the labour movement that, for the moment, we are having to live with. In 1979, 'the winter of discontent' – as some wisepen had it – I was working as a dustman in South Wales. Our crew had the Swansea areas of Townhill and Mayhill. We had a tough schedule with bins that were always either up or down stairs, and had to be returned when emptied. But the routes, the tasks were fixed, and it was *job and finish*. It was like going to the gym, we worked at speed and with luck I'd be home and washed by midday. Such a life for workers was obviously intolerable for organised capital. If such a person could work at such speed for 5-6 hours, why not make it eight. Two hours of hanging around would have been intolerable enough, the humiliation and boredom so well described in Ed Dorn's novel *By the Sound*, but there was to be none of that. More streets per crew with a small, and conditional pay raise was the result.

If conflict over intensity of labour was often partly transferred into negotiations over wages, this has also been true of the length of the working day, of overtime and how it is paid. If it is unpaid, it is a form of increased surplus value as theft. If it is paid at the normal hourly rate, it indicates the relative powerlessness of labour organisation, if it is at time-and-a-quarter or double-time, the relative strength. But unions are now listening to cases of forced overtime even where proper payment has been made. The advantage to a whole range of capital is obvious. Even if there is a pay incentive, it will be cheaper than hiring new workers or even taking on agency temps. Thus, while dockers are 'sped-up' by machinery, truck drivers are forced to work beyond the legal limits.

6 Burn out

In Chapter 10 of a remarkably pragmatic account of the British economy, Malcolm Sawyer offers an account of the intensity of labour that sounds like Marx describing the mechanics of piece-work: 'the flow of work to workers has become steadily more efficient.' We may baulk at the neutrality of 'efficiency' in this context, but he goes beyond Marx, however, in nailing down this intensity. 'The immediate factors that have generated harder work are changes in technology and work organisation augmented by information technology.' Intensity is nailed down as working harder, and that this has been increased by developments in the forces of production/productiveness of labour defined by Marx as somehow separate phenomena. Sawyer cannot nail it down quantitively, but in some 'extreme' circumstances it has stood out. Salvati describing 'rationalisation without investment' in 1960s Italy reckoned that productivity in the 1964-9 period rose at a very fast rate, as fast as in the 1950s, and yet the rate of increase in industrial investment was zero. And if Sawyer cannot make such a measurement, he is clear about its impact: 'Work intensification makes a contribution to growing productivity in

the UK economy, although its quantitive influence cannot be measured.'
It cannot be measured but he goes on to say that 'there are natural and
social limits to the extent that work can be intensified, so it is doubtful
whether further intensification is beneficial for long-term economic
growth. Moreover, there is evidence of links between work overload and
ill health, especially work-related stress, that suggests there are
substantial hidden costs even in the short-run.'

Costs to whom? Sawyer, like Professor Cooper, is assuming at least some
objective interest in worker well-being, but there is no evidence that
British business takes much interest in this type of long-term. 'The long-
term' on the cheap has been more to its taste. Historically, its strategy
has been to suck out whatever it has had going for it right down to the last
two pence, then whinge. Now, it has a government which portrays health
and safety regulations as 'red tape', as if they were the whim of pedantic
bureaucrats, jobsworths or fanatics. At the same time, 'burn-out', the
very notion of it, our picture of the speed-fed Japanese worker forty years
ago, has been expropriated by the language of genius and management
for itself.

It is both far more common and brutal than that. 'Burn-out' is indeed the
modern version of Marx's picture of capital as vampire. In a recent report
by the V.V. Giri Institute in India on call centres in that country, they talk
of graduates as cyber-coolies and note the level of burn-out due to the
intensity of labour. The Institute has its own concern about the work as
de-skilling, but has no difficulty in measuring this intensity: it is the
quota of emails and calls to be dealt with in a given time. Sawyer cannot
quantify intensity, but we can be sure that those dedicated long-hour
McKinsey folk have the templates for doing it. With its slogan that
everything can be measured, and what is measured can be managed
(Taylorism intact in the post-Fordist world), it could hardly be otherwise.
At the same time as the Institute's report, McKinsey did one of its own
which warned that, as wages rose in India and the supply of 'skilled'
workers tightened, its advantages, English language use for one, relative
to China and Eastern Europe would erode.

This threat, and its possible realisation, is a commonplace of
globalisation (the globalisation of existing power structures and relations
of production), a threat which, by sleight-of-hand, co-exists, in its own
rhetoric, with how everyone will benefit from trade liberalisation,
privatisation and selective deregulation in the long-run. In the case of
Indian call centres we can see that it is a threat used globally. The
McKinsey study highlights the matter of wages, which as described by
Marx and understood by unionised labour, cannot be abstracted from
intensity of labour struggles. In the world Marx describes, both are also
sites of national class struggles, so that he can talk of socially determined

benchmarks of intensity and wages in different countries. Despite the dynamics of globalisation of production, these benchmarks, what with the history of colonialism and its impact, remain very different in different parts of the world. In some places, there is a refusal of intensity despite wage promises, but mostly it is an involuntary situation.

It is then both unreal and unjust to compare global intensities of labour when there are such differences in wage levels. But this not-comparing doesn't preclude a clear-eyed look at some features, which are common to both intensity and wage conflicts. In the news clippings business, loyalty to fellow workers was factored in, along with a culture of frenzy that became normal. This was partly due to the time interval between first editions of the newspapers and the dawn delivery time for the packages, but more to the number of workers per shift. The small number, and thus the intensity, was justified by the existence of competition, competitive pricing and the rest.

These same pressures are – despite the huge range of wage difference – becoming globally common. Pricing oneself out of a job is a threat made even to the lowest-paid, and this 'pricing' factors in the level of intensity. It takes different forms and comes to the same thing, speed-up, downsizing, it all comes down to working harder in a given time. At the same time, the most primitive Taylorism imaginable has been given a new lease of life by technologies of surveillance. Call centres have gained some notoriety for the policing of toilet breaks, the random listening in to check performance and so on, but it goes far wider than that. Modern technologies allow capital to check where each worker is at any given time, and in many cases, what he/she has been doing at any given moment.

7 Fit in or stand up for yourself

Milan Kundera has described how, post the 1968 invasion, many Czech dissidents managed to get certain 'manual jobs', and found them liberating. You could stay out of trouble without compromising your integrity, and the work by its very repetition without the intensity, allowed a freedom to think. Such jobs, I suspect, are thin on the ground these days, especially in the modern Czech Republic, still less in Slovakia, which is taking on a China-like bogeyman image for Western workers and perhaps even Indian ones, too. There is no freedom to think in a call centre.

Instead, we get management gurus talking of how 'passionate employees get better results' as quoted by Madeleine Bunting in *Willing Slaves*. Passionate?! As young English Situationists, we found stories of company mass prayers or mass exhortations, mainly Japanese, both funny and scary, and imagined dissident workers taking the piss. Now such things are just plain scary and have a strong whiff of fundamentalism. There is no room for dissidents at Asda or Orange, Bunting tells us. Their managements, and others like them, aim to use the concepts of brand loyalty and teamwork to give meaning to peoples' lives, she says. Various opinion polls like that from the Penna Consultancy, purport to show the general success of such strategies: that there is greater 'loyalty, creativity and productivity' from employees who find 'meaning' in their work. Meaning?! All this, while it is also a commonplace that there are no jobs for life, there being no reciprocal loyalty.

This characteristic at least is equally true of the privileged sector of immaterial labour described by Lazzarato. Privileged it is, but often working on short-term contracts. It is the privileged version of the outrageous super-exploitation of workers permanently on call, but paid only for the hours worked. At the BBC, six-month contracts are common; at *The Guardian's* small film documentary offshoot, two months, though this is better at least than month-by-month contracts being enforced by Group4 Securicor in South Africa. For people with special talents in this privileged sector and with very high earning power, such a system is not stressful, but further down the production chain of even such privileged labour, the next job is not guaranteed.

Instead, on each job the mantra that 'passionate employees get the best results' is the norm, even when this is not true. It is not enough to produce a graphic in which a globe spins round to show Bob Geldof's face on one side and a map of Africa on the other, competently and without fuss. No, you are also required to believe that it is of the greatest importance. There is an intensity of labour in this sector that requires of you that you believe it, and show that you believe it. And in this small world, word gets around. You have to 'fit in' as McKinsey says of its people: you can be as clever as clever can be, work those heroic long hours, but you've also got to fit in.

In the privileged sector of commodified cultural production, cocaine has proved to be the ideal drug in that it produces an intensity of importance, of 'passion' about whatever is in front of it, and the long hours of concentration needed to make something of it, and a likely disregard of the length of the working day and how it may continue into your official not-working time. It may be losing its exclusive cachet as news comes in of Derbyshire commuters snorting the stuff, but it does have these qualities. Amphetamine, with its tendency to endless digression would be quite unsuitable for such work, whereas its cheapness in comparison to cocaine (of the order of 1:12), and its chemical qualities make it ideal for long hours of low-paid repetitive factory work.

The disparities in wages and incomes, and the consumption possibilities they afford (drugs and otherwise), make proclamations of the unity of labour resistance to the dictates of capital facile. This does not mean that international solidarities are not, nor cannot, be forged. At the same, in many parts of the Western World, unity is undermined by increasing inequality, and this rise in inequality is in large part due to the weakening of trade unions. This weakening has been caused not just by rapid technological change and globalisation, but by persistent government legislation to this end. Its impact was clearly seen in the UK in last year's Gate Gourmet strike. Everyone working for a wage should be in a trade union. Easy to say, and made very difficult in practice, but there is a greater chance of success if certain cultural/ideological battles are fought with vigour.

At its most general, the claims of neo-liberalism and governments ideologically committed to it, to be modern or modernising (something especially important in the UK where each move New Labour makes to the most archaic view of the world is presented as modernising) has to be challenged on that ground. Its presentation of trade unions as dinosaurs is laughable. Compare the Respect festivals (not the Galloway/SWP party) initiated by the unions, which did reflect modern multiracial London, with New Labour's Dome and its risible Cool Britannia. For the more privileged sectors of immaterial labour, such a challenge demands the *re-creation of proletarian values, most of all that, whatever else, you go to work for the wage, and never mind the flim-flam*. Despite a failure to unionise, this at least was a shared point-of-view of news clippings workers, and we forced the introduction of a new shift system that greatly reduced the length of the working month.

More recently, an example has been given by scriptwriters working for Fox TV on reality TV shows in the USA. It may be hard to have much sympathy for the writers on reality TV shows (or with workers for Group4 Securicor), but that is beside the point. We don't know if cocaine was part of their diet, but it is said they were being forced to skip meals, submit fake time cards and work more than 80 hours a week. Now with the backing of the Writers Guild they are taking legal action, as are other writers, against other TV companies. Zachary Isenberg, one of the plaintiffs in the Fox lawsuit complied with much of this, because he was keen to get on in television. But, he said: 'I spend almost my entire waking time at work. I enjoy my job and want to keep doing it, but I also know there comes a certain point where you have to stand up for yourself.'

Previously published in: *Mute Magazine*, 07/03/2006; also available at:
http://www.metamute.org/en/Intensities-of-Labour-from-Amphetamine-to-Cocaine

Pedagogy of Human Capital

By Stewart Martin

What is the relation of education to capitalism today? And what are the consequences for an emancipatory education? These questions might seem less bold than bald, untextured by the currency of popular debate. Yet they are unavoidable, and not just for the European Social Democracies in the process of negotiating the commodification of their welfare provision, but also for all those confronting the neo-liberal restructuring of what used to be considered beyond the market. There is equally a sense in which these questions are both obscured and entrenched by the difficulties in answering them, theoretically as well as practically. Besides the formidable noise of specificities that tends to drown them out, the scene of contemporary education presents striking ambivalences.

On the one hand, there has been an exponential and seemingly inevitable expansion of the realm of formal education, that is, education that leads to publicly recognised qualifications, both in the expansion of the traditional sector of schools, colleges and universities, and in the incorporation of new sectors. This is evident in the rise of student numbers, the extended total length of study, accompanied by the increase in post-graduate degrees, as well as the repeated drives to establish 'vocational' qualifications or the formal ratification of what previously would have been considered apprenticeships or such like. McDegrees did not come out of the blue. The evolution of education as a leisure sector is also notable, as is the growth of educational initiatives within the leisure industries. (This may sound like the privilege of the rich West or North speaking, but even in more impoverished countries, who is seeking to delimit education?) On the other hand, this expansion of education is comparatively informal, both in the sense that it takes place through new sectors that are outside the traditional institutions and their rules, and in that education as a whole has become in certain respects informalised. 'Distance learning', 'work-based learning', 'home-based learning', 'lifelong learning', all indicate the integration of education into realms previously considered outside the school gates. The internet has been instrumental in these developments. The emphasis on 'transferable skills' is also indicative of how various disciplines' rigour has been somewhat suspended or re-qualified. But these expansions, whether formal or informal, stand in contrast to certain pervasive contractions of education. Efficiency is the name of the game, with reduced resources per student the supreme goal, both from the side of provision and from the supplements students must contribute. The rich can buy more resources, but not another goal.

Of course, many of these phenomena and their apparent conflicts can be understood as a direct consequence of commodification. This is certainly fundamental, but what form does this take exactly? Stacking high and selling cheap only accounts for part of these developments. It doesn't explain their ideological function, which draws on certain emancipatory claims. The liberation of 'choice' and 'opportunity' is usually the carrot; the stick is the threat of deserved poverty, whether of the individual or the nation. It is all too clear that education has become a way for rich nations to manage class conflicts, either through keeping people off the unemployment register, or through seducing their populations into the idea that they can all be middle class, with proletarianisation becoming an attribute of newly industrialised nations like China or India, or immigrant work forces. Within this ideology, failure is educational failure. The idea that contemporary education is characterised by the move away from authoritarian forms of indoctrination and towards forms of self-directed or autonomous learning is perhaps the most powerful emancipatory ideology in this context. 'Lifelong learning' is exemplary. The phrase oscillates between the dream of fulfilling self-transformation beyond the privileges of youth, and the nightmare of indiscriminate de-skilling and re-skilling according to the dictates of a 'flexible' labour market. It modifies the ideology of meritocracy, which is perhaps the core educational ideology through which the contradictions of capitalism and democracy are recoded as the successes and (more usually) 'failures' of disciplined individualism: 'lifelong learning' extends 'meritocracy' to the whole of your life. Qualification is a receding horizon; its promise of maturity takes the form of infantalisation.

Many of these educational phenomena coalesce in the socio-political characterisations that have gained increasingly insistent currency since the 1960s: post-industrial society, neo-liberalism, cognitive capitalism, immaterial labour, bio-politics. The socio-economic qualities indicated by these terms – the emphasis on white collar labour and the service economy, and the significance of high-tech knowledge and its socio-economic relations or networks; the deregulation of labour markets, making labour more pliable to the demands of markets; the commodification of areas of society traditionally considered outside the economy or market, extending the demands of the production and reproduction of labour power to all aspects of social and natural life; the demand for increased self-discipline and initiative, if not creativity, in wage labour; and the emergence of new terms of political struggle and dispute over capitalism and its limits – all provide an increasingly familiar context for articulating the transforming pressures on education today. Indeed, it is evident that education is at the core of these formations. Just as we can draw parallels between the traditional school and the factory, so we can between the dispersal of the factory into society as a whole and the dispersal of the school. The expansion of education is the conduit for the transformation of wage labour, entwined with the procurement of a new kind of labourer and even, some would say, a new kind of human being. Gary S. Becker won the Nobel Prize in economics for his study of 'human capital', understood as the economic value of educational qualifications.[1] The term has since acquired a bio-capitalist currency, standing at the centre of political-philosophical disputes over the commodification of human beings. Rather than the capitalisation of education, it has come to indicate the educationalisation of capital.

These developments have led to a crisis of ideas of emancipatory education. Not merely because they have become embattled, but due to their appropriation and instrumentalisation. John Dewey's critique of 'traditional' education – its dependence on the authoritarian discipline of the teacher, and his defence of 'progressives' taking a non-hierarchical approach to pedagogy, embedding learning within a shared social context, and thereby integrating education into a democratic ethos, committed to the 'quality of experience' – sounds commonplace today, but also naïve about the entwinement of this education within new labour markets.[2] Paulo Freire's inspirational 'Pedagogy of the Oppressed', despite its direct confrontation with capitalism as a class struggle of master and slave, remains similarly remote in its articulation of the relation of teacher-master to pupil-slave in a way that is removed from the expanded and self-directed context of the new educational forms.[3] Jean-François Lyotard's reports on the postmodern condition of education does manage to articulate many of these forms and their relation to new forms of wage labour, but he is led to profoundly ambivalent conclusions. His claim that, '[w]e should be happy that the tendency toward the temporary contract is ambiguous: it is not totally subordinated to the goal of the system, yet the system tolerates it', is precarious, if not desperate.[4] The ambivalences of this situation are well recognised by many commentators, but they remain. Perhaps this merely indicates that we face a situation that cannot be theoretically resolved, and that theoretical criticism can at best aspire to clarification of the terms of political engagement.

It seems that the root of this ambivalence concerns the way in which the new forms of wage labour require forms of self-directed skills and competences that have previously been considered the preserve of progressive education, namely, its focus on authoritarian and autonomous modes of pedagogy. In short, the autonomy aspired to by emancipatory education has turned out to involve points of indifference to the autonomy required of new capitalist work. This has profound implications. Crucially, it is entwined with fundamental transformations at stake in the relation of capitalism to life. If education has become the means through which advanced capitalist societies extend the subsumption of labour under capital to the subsumption of all aspects of social life, then the issue of emancipatory education needs to be understood in terms of this radical alteration to capitalism's metabolism.

So, if we ask what an emancipatory education should be today, we are led to questions about changes in the basic structure of capital. This may sound reductive to those seeking a stronger independence of educational concerns from economic matters, but this independence must be wrested from out of the social fact of this reduction. Moreover, there is a reverse determination revealed here, of capitalism itself as an educational form, a pedagogy.

Educating life

Core pedagogical concepts and forms, such as 'rule', 'freedom', 'subject', 'autonomy', and so on, are already involved in capitalism's fundamental antagonistic relation between capital and living labour, where capital exploits the powers of living labour, appropriating the production of surplus value. Capital aspires to autonomy in this relation; a self-valorisation in which it creates its own value, reducing labour to its rule and its interiority. The subjection of living labour makes capital subject, indeed sovereign. Capital, not the consumer, is king. This is expressed in the contractual agreement of a person, who, as such, is assumed to be free and able to sell their labour as their property, becoming a wage labourer through which their capacities are expropriated. But capital, for Marx at least, is ultimately incapable of autonomy. It remains intrinsically dependent on living labour, which is actually creative of value. Autonomy is rather the potential of living labour, not capital. The struggle of labour against capital is therefore a struggle against the rule of capital, against labour's external or heteronymous determination by capital, and for labour's self-determination, its autonomy.

The educational consequences of this account are various and conflictual, but also profound, extending well beyond the classroom and its textbooks. From the development and dissemination of knowledge about capitalism, and the formation and discipline of 'the party', to the more devolved and self-directed activities of labourers and anti-capitalists – pedagogical issues suffuse this terrain. The deep conflicts between science and ideology, party and proletariat, etc., remain all too familiar today, even though their early forms have decayed. The pedagogy of the oppressed, as Paulo Freire showed, reveals a disputed lesson at the heart of this whole formation: the emancipation of the oppressed from their masters must avoid reproducing new masters, 'emancipators' who invert emancipation into a new form of oppression.

The reproduction of class struggle within the communist movement may seem like an arcane problem, something resolved by the more 'horizontal' organisation of recent anti-capitalist movements, but it is a problem that persists in new guises. Moreover, while its solution promises a simplified struggle of slaves against masters, the struggle against capitalism is not so easily personified, especially today.

This returns us to the pedagogical structure of capital itself, about which Freire among others has surprising little to say. The terms of this are in some sense plain: capital functions as a master, subjecting living labour to its rule, the law of value, in the process of its self-valorisation; emancipation demands a counter-pedagogy, disobeying the law of value, enabling living labour to have value for itself. The struggle of labour against capital thus assumes an educational ambition and vice versa, an emancipatory pedagogy of autonomy.

But returning to the ABC of capitalism does not only face the subsequent task of elaboration and specification. It also enables the exposure of deep transformations in the evolution of capitalism, which have equally profound effects for any pedagogy of autonomy. What is at stake here is the intensification of capital's subsumption of labour – extending it beyond the industrial restructuring of labour processes diagnosed by Marx, and even beyond his discernment of an expanded realm of productive labour that incorporates various social and scientific supplements of the labour process – to the subsumption by capital of life itself. In other words, the colonisation by capital of all those aspects of living labour that were previously deemed outside the labour process, from leisure and the environment, to sex and physiology, and certainly education. The consequences for the struggle against capitalism are self-evidently profound: the dissipation, if not outright negation, of the basic antagonism between living labour and capital.

The contention that capitalism has subsumed living labour may be exaggerated. Few stand by it unequivocally. But it is plausible to consider it as the regulative idea of a number of theories of late capitalism. Furthermore, it is possible to understand it as the source of a series of profound political disputes between Right and Left. On the Right, these tend to concern the market's legitimate intrusion into the realms of nationhood, religion, familial life, etc. On the left, they tend to concern the very possibility of a non-capitalist life; insofar as this seems impossible, its disputes tend to retreat to liberal versions of drawing the market's boundaries.

What is particularly revealing and significant here, certainly for the radical Left, is the intense ambivalence that the contention of capital's subsumption of life has produced within neo- and post-Marxist thought.

On the one hand, there is the understandably pessimistic reaction, from the Frankfurt School to Baudrillard, that tends to see the intensification of capitalist subsumption as an incorporation of all social and natural life within the reproduction of capitalism, leading to the exhaustion of anti-capitalist politics, even its imagination. Notoriously, environmental catastrophe seems a far more realistic future for many than an end to capitalism. On the other hand, Negri and others have drawn a radically opposed conclusion: that capital's tendency to subsume life is merely a consequence of the intensification of capital's parasitic dependence on life; that capitalist production processes change not of their own accord, but as a result of the power and resistance of labour. This, therefore, demonstrates the very creativity and growing autonomy of living labour, which capital only subsumes as an increasingly thin membrane of control, predisposed to disintegrate. For the former, capital tends to subsume not only labour, but life; for the latter, capital's tendency to subsume life is merely its tendency to reach its unsubsumable limit. Such opposed reactions to such similar structural characterisations of capital is striking. It indicates an intractable disagreement, since both reactions seem liable to each other's objections. But rather than approaching it as a simple choice or alternative, perhaps it indicates a change of the terms of struggle that needs to be grasped as such: no longer between living labour and capital, as Marx understood this, where capital is understood simply as dead or mechanical; but between alternative forms of life, capitalist life versus non-capitalist life. In other words, not a struggle between life and non-life, but between alternative forms of life. Negri remains an orthodox Marxist in maintaining a residual, unsubsumable, border between capital and life – non-capitalist life remains for him a tautology. The Frankfurt School's thinking of non-capitalist life tended to remain utopian. Neither of them quite confront the predicament that anti-capitalism has become the struggle to wrest non-capitalist life from capitalist life.

This predicament also suggests a change in the significance of the aspiration to the autonomy of living labour. If both capitalist life and non-capitalist life tend to autonomy, then non-capitalist life must be understood according to an alternative form of autonomy. Indeed, given this issue, perhaps the value of autonomy should be revised? Perhaps living labour's heteronomy should be sought as resistant to the autonomy of capitalist life? But how would this advance on labour's heteronomous determination by capital according to Marx's original characterisation? The terms may spiral here, but this speculation is not idle.

The consequences for education are profound and in many respects very visible. Most obviously, the subsumption of life by capital offers a powerful explanation of why education, despite being formally outside the labour process, is nonetheless treated as integral to it, indeed, an urgent and necessary part of the capitalist mode of production. By the same token, it also suggests that the extension of education beyond the formal realms of schools, colleges, etc., should also be seen within this extended orbit of production. In sum, it provides grounds for understanding the subsumption of education by capital, and indicates how education itself becomes a mode, perhaps the central mode, of capital's subsumption of life. 'Lifelong learning' is not exhausted by this explanation, but it can certainly be interpreted as a struggle between capitalist life and non-capitalist life.

But, what of an emancipatory education? Clearly its terms become questionable. If capital can no longer be understood as a mechanical rule that oppresses living labour's autonomy from outside it, then the powerful correspondence this has to a pedagogy of emancipation, as a struggle of autonomy, contra dogmatic rules, is problematised, if not inverted. If life can be subsumed by the law of value, such that it is life's own law, its autonomy, then does this not suggest that a new pedagogy is called for?

If these queries are substantive then they indicate a crisis for the terms of an emancipatory education. But they are difficult to resolve. Perhaps this indicates that they should be treated as the issues of a novel struggle between capitalist life and non-capitalist life fought out on an expanded field of education.

Autonomy or heteronomy?

In order to try and clarify this transformation of terms it is worth considering the broader context of their evolution – in particular, the libertarian and egalitarian formation of the idea of autonomy that emerges with the modern notion of democracy, and that in large part defines the idea and significance of emancipatory education. The French Revolution grounded freedom on equality, as an inalienable right, introduced in the form or guise of 'man', and therefore distinguished its notion of democracy from the aristocratic forms of antiquity. This introduced a non-dogmatic conception of law: freedom must be subject to universal law, demonstrating its equality, but this law must simultaneously be subject to freedom, demonstrating that it is not a new enslavement. This dialectic of subjection infuses the idea of autonomy: a rule to which a subject subjects 'himself'. Obedience is therefore transformed into an act of freedom. In consequence, one is not subject to dogmatic or externally imposed rules – heteronomy.

This idea of autonomy produces a crisis and reinvention of the idea of education. For, insofar as education is essentially a relation of subjection – of student by master – then it is incompatible with the constitution of autonomy. Even if education means merely the transmission of something from those who have it to those who do not, how can there be an education in autonomy? How can autonomy be 'received' without collapsing it into subjection? Autonomy would rather need to be an egalitarian presupposition of any such exchange. If education contradicts autonomy, then it should be left behind in the seminary, or reduced to a minor and subordinate cultural function.

These contradictions justified the various forms of anti-education to emerge from this epoch, frequently attached to the natural, the naïve and the untrained or perhaps self-trained. And yet this anti-education also induced new ideas of education, of an education against education, which might indeed succeed as an education in autonomy. Rousseau's *Emile, or On Education* has his Savoyard vicar profess a faith in 'common reason' to his young companion, rather than conduct 'learned speeches or profound reasonings':

> I do not want to argue with you or even convince you. [...] Reason is common to us, and we have the same interest in listening to it.'[5]

Kant, famously enthused by this peculiar education, conceives of enlightenment as a matter of courage: 'Have courage to use your own understanding!' Further:

> Rules and formulas, those mechanical aids to the rational use, or rather misuse, of [man's] natural gifts, are the shackles of a permanent immaturity.[6]

The paradox of Joseph Jacotot's universal method of teaching is exemplary: 'I must teach you that I have nothing to teach you.'[7]

The paradox of an education in autonomy should not be overstated, since, if freedom should be subject to equality – albeit as much as vice versa – then education's subjecting function might be employed to this end. Still, this only tends to heighten the tensions that remain precariously in balance in the idea of autonomy. If one becomes free through subjecting oneself to oneself, then there is an obvious sense in which freedom is understood in essentially disciplinary terms, as if doubling subjection cancelled it out, emancipating a subject, rather than just oppressing it twice over. The conception of freedom in terms of autonomy thereby articulates freedom as a function of ruling, freedom as domination. Autodidact: the educational hero of autonomy is well named. It may be insisted that the unity of equality and freedom in autonomy is essentially and necessarily antagonistic, as the unity of competing rules. But this doesn't sound like a good life.

An antidote to this antagonism was found in a rapprochement with nature and life, often via art. This is even the case in Kant, despite his tendency to express autonomy in disciplinary terms, and it was already central to Rousseau. Schiller's letters *On the Aesthetic Education of Man* (1795) is a manifesto of the new pedagogy at stake here. The beautiful artwork presents autonomy less in terms of self-ruling or self-domination, than in the suspension of rules. The whole disciplinary ethos of giving or receiving rules is displaced by play. Art becomes that through which the antagonism of nature and reason is mediated: nature's heteronomy, its externality to human reason, is internalised through art, but without dominating it; hence art presents a way through which reason can relate to human nature without dominating it. Autonomy is then rendered a form of life. This aesthetic conception of autonomy, of a life that is spirit, infuses speculative philosophy from Fichte to Hegel, and is pivotal to the theoretical founding of the influential University of Berlin between 1807 and 1810.

This formation of spirit assumes a profoundly ambivalent relationship to Marx's diagnosis of capitalism. In one sense, Hegel's speculative idealism provides the model for articulating the speculative character of capital as self-valorising value. However, Marx's idea that living labour should free itself from its determination by the dogmatic and mechanical rule of capital – and not just as brute nature – clearly remains indebted to key aspects of a speculative concept of life.

These equivocations are reproduced when we consider the extension of capital's subsumption of labour to that of life in general. Marx's modelling of capital on the speculative concept is simultaneously critical of it, in that he draws a limit to the idea's/capital's subsumptive capacities. But if these capacities exceed these limits in late capitalism then this overcomes Marx's critique, and speculative idealism becomes true in a sense that neither he nor the idealists claimed: a model of the subsumption of life under capital, of capitalist life.

In so far as this is substantive, the whole project of an education in autonomy, even where this takes radically anti-dogmatic and aesthetic forms, becomes problematic, if not undermined, as a simple alternative to capitalism. This justifies the attempt to try and conceive of anti-capitalism through alternatives to autonomy, re-valuing forms of anti-autonomy or heteronomy. This would not only radicalise the aesthetic mediations proposed by Schiller, but exceed them. (This is the alternative sought by Lyotard among others, overcoming Adorno's hesitations.) But anti-autonomy is scarcely a straightforward alternative.

Its advocates tend to buy into a neo-vitalism (Deleuze is seminal here) which ironically returns us to Marx's investment in living labour as essentially independent from capital, and thereby to the same problem of living labour's subsumption by late capitalism. Otherwise, a more intensive naturalism is sought out that tends to be indifferent to the subjection of humans and just as indifferent about capitalist culture. It is perhaps unsurprising that in this context an alternative form of heteronomy has also gained ground: a neo-dogmatic anti-capitalism that reconceives of forms of subjection as forms of political subjectivity. (Žižek's and Badiou's alternative Lacanian-Leninisms are illustrative.) These projects are far from escaping the ambivalences of autonomy; frequently, they simply reproduce them.

The contemporary polemics between autonomy and heteronomy may be complex, but the polemic persists. And while the opponents often fight it out within the Left, its stakes traverse the political spectrum. The claim here is simply that these disputes should be interpreted in terms of the effects of the subsumption of life under capital, and the struggle this produces between capitalist life and non-capitalist life. So we return, by way of another route, to the same junction reached before.

And what of education? The effects have already been forecast, but the issues are modified. Should an emancipatory education be understood as a form of self-determination, or as freedom from self-determination? Should it be free of subjection, or an alternative subjection? Should education be a determination of life, or an emancipation from life's determination? Autonomy or heteronomy? It is difficult to answer these questions, and not just because they are abstract. But whatever the answers may be, for them to constitute an emancipatory education within advanced capitalist societies today, they must engage in the struggle to wrest non-capitalist life from capitalist life.

Footnotes:

[1] Gary S. Becker, *Human Capital: A Theoretical and Empirical Analysis, with Special Reference to Education*, Chicago and London: University of Chicago Press, 1964, 3rd edition 1993. Becker won the Nobel Memorial Prize in Economic Science in 1992.

[2] See John Dewey's *Democracy and Education* (1916), New York: Free Press, 1966, and *Experience and Education*, (1938), New York: Touchstone, 1997.

[3] See Paulo Freire's *Pedagogy of the Oppressed* (1968), trans. M. Bergman Ramos, London and New York, Continuum, 2000.

[4] Jean-François Lyotard, *The Postmodern Condition: A Report on Knowledge* (1979), trans G. Bennington and B. Massumi, Manchester University Press, 1984, p. 66.

[5] Jean-Jacques Rousseau, *Emile, or On Education* (1762), trans. Allan Bloom, Basic Books, 1979, p. 266.

[6] Immanuel Kant, "An Answer to the Question: What is Enlightenment?" (1784), in *Perpetual Peace and Other Essays on Politics, History and Moral Practice*, trans. Ted Humphrey, Hackett, Indianapolis and Cambridge, 1983, p. 41.

[7] Quoted in J.S. Van de Weyer, *Sommaire des leçons publiques de M. Jacotot sur les principes de l'enseignement universel*, Brussels, 1822, p. 11, itself quoted in Jacques Rancière, *The Ignorant Schoolmaster: Five Lessons in Intellectual Emancipation*, trans. Kristin Ross, Stanford: Stanford University Press, 1991, p. 15.

Previously published in: *Mute Magazine,* Vol. 2, No. 8, Spring 2008, pp. 32-45. Also available at: http://www.metamute.org/en/Pedagogy-of-Human-Capital

This essay draws some ideas and phrases from a previous essay, "An Aesthetic Education Against Aesthetic Education", *Radical Philosophy*, 141, Jan/Feb 2007, written as part of the journal's contribution to the Documenta 12 "Magazines Project", in particular its theoretical motif, "What is to be done? (Education)", which is also available on the Documenta 12 website:
http://magazines.documenta.de/frontend/article.php?IdLanguage=1&NrArticle=1504

Recomposing the University

By Tiziana Terranova & Marc Bousquet

Far removed from the clichéd image of the 'ivory tower', today's universities have been opened to the harsh realities of neoliberal economics: huge volumes of students, extreme levels of performance-geared management, casualisation of employment, and the conversion of students into 'consumers'. In the name of democratisation and equality, the university has become a cross between a supermarket and a factory whose consumers are also its hyper-exploited labour force. Here, in an email exchange, Marc Bousquet and Tiziana Terranova, themselves employed in US and British universities respectively, describe the way the system works from the inside and look at the possibilities for getting out of it. Far from being a simple question of domination, they contend, the conditions of 'mass intellectuality' – also shared by many knowledge workers elsewhere in the 'social factory' – create enormous scope for new alliances and forms of resistance.

Tiziana Terranova: I think it would be good to start with the 'big picture', that is how the university is an open system opening onto the larger field of casualised and underpaid 'socialised labour power'. The latter is also often referred to as 'mass intellectuality' or even networked intelligence (an abstract quality of social labour power as it becomes increasingly informational and communicative). I have been thinking about it in terms of the opening up of disciplinary institutions as described by Deleuze in his essay on control societies. I would like to move from the idea that the university is some kind of ivory tower or a self-enclosed institution whose current state and future concerns a minority of professionals to that of the university as part of the 'diffuse factory' as described in Autonomist work. I think that their description of a shift from a society where production takes place predominantly in the closed site of the factory to one where it is the whole of society that is turned into a factory – a productive site – is still very fitting politically. But in fact, the debate seems to be stuck in the false opposition between the static, sheltered ivory tower and the dynamic, democratic market.

Marc Bousquet: You're right to call it a false opposition, since the university has never been a shelter from either commerce or politics. And yet the nostalgic idea of the university as a 'refuge' from social life is amazingly persistent, isn't it? The reality is very different. Especially in the U.S., where nearly 60 percent of high school graduates have some experience of 'higher ed', it should be obvious that the university is part of the social factory. The problem is that it's the wrong kind of factory.

TT: Maybe.

MB: Anyway, it seems that the ivory tower myth persists, because it has so many useful functions. For intellectuals, as well as many artists and activists, the idea of the university as a refuge often gives them the feeling of Archimedes – as if it offered a stable fulcrum from which they can move the earth itself. For others, the ivory tower image is a kind of smokescreen for the double-talk and structural transformations of neo-liberalism, a chastity belt as the Bush-Thatcher-Clinton-Blair bloc leads it to market: 'the university is too much of an ivory tower – we have to make it practical' on the one hand, and on the other hand: 'because the university is so much of an ivory tower, we can trust that its profit-seeking will be benevolent.' It signifies all the way around the political clock. Really, 'ivory tower' is the classic ideologeme – practically un-dislodgeable from any point of view.

TT: So the university is no longer, simply, an ivory tower (although I am sure that even the ivory tower persists in pockets of isolated privilege, too), but it has not simply turned into a 'market' or 'supermarket' either – providing exciting new courses/services to discriminating student-customers in search of that elusive perfect value-for-money combination. If anything, it is another site of implosion of the modern separation between consumption, production and reproduction.

MB: Yes, the sense of 'separate' circuits is quickly eroding. And 'supermarket,' as opposed to 'market,' is perfect. It goes beyond the nostalgia of the market-as-agora or public sphere to capture the sense of total commodification.

Once we see that the campus is seamlessly part of the whole (social and global) factory floor – in this sense an unprivileged location in a vast horizontal plane – it becomes an opportunity for the self-organisation of labour, and just as you say, reorganising the social relations of re/production. But in my mind, that would mean giving up the fantasy of the fulcrum, of the ivory tower model in which the university offers a 'safe space' to benevolent 'directors of the transformation,' operating in a cloud-circled meta-plane for mental labourers. For the university to become a site of worker self-organisation and the reproduction of an oppositional mentality – much less the catalyst of a radicalised Multitude or 'mass intellectuality' – it would mean operating in an unsafe manner.

TT: In your writings on US academic labour, you emphasise the increasing polarisation between tenured academics (of which many exercise mainly administrative/managerial functions of 'directors of transformation') and a large casualised teaching force of graduate students and temporary workers.

MB: Tenured faculty schizophrenically experience themselves as both labour and management, a contradictory position reflected in US labour law. They also have another schizophrenia of seeking to produce or direct a cultural-material transformation, while simultaneously serving capital (as reproductive labour) through the socialisation of a disciplined professional-managerial class.

Getting beyond either schizophrenia is a hazardous project that ultimately threatens the faculty's 'directorial' position. In the US, for instance, more than half of the tenured faculty in public higher education are unionised. This is not impressive by European standards, but it's three times the average level of worker organisation in the US I bring it up, because – with a few exceptions – it has thus far been very much an old-style craft unionism, a labour aristocracy that preserves workplace hierarchy, and has been very much complicit in the perma-temping of the university workforce, preserving their own jobs, while selling out the future. While those unions are moving slowly to address casualisation, the kind of dramatic change implicit in the notion of a mass intellectuality or even the smaller fraction of mental labourers off the campus, would really imply a reverse of the trajectory we usually imagine: not, 'how can the university serve as a platform for changing society on behalf of the casualised,' but 'how can the casualised hijack the university in their own interest?'

This dictatorship of the flexible would not be a safe process for the tenured who imagine themselves as directors of transformation and safely above the fray.

TT: Yes, and this reversal does not necessarily need to concern only university staff, but it must somehow construct an immanent connection to the masses of students who are increasingly going through higher education.

MB: Yes, absolutely.

TT: I find what is happening in the UK with higher education very interesting from this point of view. As you might be aware, the UK system has been through a turbulent decade. In most areas, budgets have been cut back or frozen for a number of years, while student numbers have increased exponentially (for example, according to UCAS statistics the number of accepted first year students has risen from 300,000 in 1996 to almost 370,000 in 2002 – an increase of 25 percent in just six years).

The UK higher education system has gone from being a manageable cottage industry more or less autonomously run with a moderate number of students living more or less well on a grant system, to something that in places really looks like mass higher education –

without the grants and with a new system of fees. There is obviously much to be said about this process.

MB: More like the US model. Wide access, but fee-for-service. Though there was a period in which the largest US public systems – in New York and California – were both open-access and tuition free (or nearly free).

TT: Many students are going into higher education because they think that they have no choice in terms of their future occupational opportunities and they have been told that in spite of the massive debts that they will be likely to incur, higher education is, after all, a good investment in terms of future earnings. There is this weird conjuring trick where they are really 'sold' this image of themselves as customers in the university supermarket, while for many of them the reality is that they are working in supermarkets, hospitals and temping in offices to pay for their maintenance while they are studying.

MB: Exactly right. Being a student is ideologically attached to the idea of 'leisure' when in reality it's increasingly visible as a way of being hyper-exploited as a temp worker.

TT: On top of all this work, they will also get a 'good' start in life by learning to live with debt and there will be a good deal of that in their future life. Thus, while they are addressed as customers, they appear to me to be, in many cases, very far away from the model of the spoiled student or the education customer. They are working twice as hard as their predecessors to support themselves through their studies; while working they accumulate debts which they will have to work hard to pay back once they graduate, in an accumulation of interest rates that ranges from credit cards to personal loans to mortgages. There aren't really very many student-customers, are there? It seems to me that it is production through and through.

What I wonder is what this mass of students is doing to higher education?

MB: You mean that they are changing the system by inhabiting it.

TT: Yes, I think that it is an exciting transformation and does not necessarily need to be interpreted as a 'dumbing down'. On the contrary, the entry of such a mass of students into higher education implies a political transformation in the role of the university – its reinvention, so to speak. The ways in which this transformation is being managed over here is totally predictable and unsurprising. On the one hand, there is a heightened level of top down, managerial, informational control – an endless, centralised output of new guidelines, targets and initiatives, which introduce post-industrial management into the old guild-like university system and which in many cases is pushing teaching staff workloads to extreme limits.

On the student side, although stratified, the UK system is still in a turbulent phase of growth which means that 'new' and for many suspicious degrees (such as media studies) are over-recruiting, while older disciplines from mathematics to engineering are suffering. This lack of synchronicity between the degree market and the labour market is obviously a result of the interference of desire in what should be a 'rational' economic choice (thus undermining the notion of the rationality of the working class as an internal variable of capital, as Negri once put it). What seems to most concern the higher education managers, however, is not this lack of relation between the labour market and the degree market. They seem to be more concerned with preserving hierarchical differences between universities, degrees, and ultimately social classes.

MB: So the massification of higher ed represents an opportunity for transformation (and I guess you mean to indicate a pretty wide field of possibility, not just for a tighter fit between study and labour markets). But management is responding aggressively to contain the opportunity?

TT: There is an attempt to restrain the turbulence and instability introduced by rising student numbers by engineering a differential system of value – one that would be able to clearly distinguish, for example, prestigious institutions (an Ivy League) from their less prestigious, but still reputable peers (red brick universities), from a bottom layer of vocationally-oriented, hands-on, working class not-quite-universities (ex-polytechnics). This is why we are going from the 'star' system of evaluation (where different departments get a number of stars depending on performance at the research assessment exercise) to a 'league' system. Apparently there were too many high ratings and not enough of a sense of 'value-difference'. A league system will thus be introduced allowing a fine-graded hierarchisation of university degrees and research environments. The underlying idea is that 'excellence' can only be produced through a concentration of resources (including the best students) which goes against a great deal of what we know about 'knowledge ecologies', for example. An American colleague has suggested that here, too, the model is the United States where higher education has always been solidly stratified.

MB: Yes. More so every year.

TT: So I wanted to ask you about your experience. In which ways have the discourse and technologies of managerialism and privatisation interacted with the ferocious educational hierarchies that we know are a feature of the US higher education system?

MB: That's a great question. There's at least two issues here – the ranking of campuses against each other, and the role of higher education as a system in reproducing the 'ferocious hierarchies' of class relations in the US and globally (which still remain largely invisible to the US population).

The increasingly fine-grained ranking of campuses against each other is most important to the upper fractions of the professional-managerial class, for whom the ideology of the US as a 'classless meritocracy' remains partly viable (a fraction that includes most higher education faculty themselves, as well as media professionals, many lawyers and physicians, etc.). With the intensification of the ranking, the percentage of persons who feel that the 'meritocracy' is working appears to shrink. That realisation is probably a good thing overall. For instance, the appearance of graduate employee union movements at Ivy League campuses over the past 20 years (Yale, Columbia, Penn, Brown, Cornell) reflects in part the collapsing viability of merit ideology even while the 'rank' of schools against each other gains ever greater 'cultural capital.' The problem is that the 'cultural capital,' while real, is relative. The rank of schools acquires more relative value, because overall the 'cultural capital' disseminated by schooling has become scarcer in some way that it's important for us to try to understand.

TT: Do you see any consistent strategy or tactical manoeuvres through which such cultural capital is made scarce and then given a value?

MB: Well, the classic strategy of creating a 'surplus' of workers that has finally hit the American and European professional-managerial class, and the expansion of higher ed – not just internally, but globally – is a big part of that, isn't it? The US business papers have been full of panicky articles about the 'new' outsourcing 'crisis' of white-collar work (engineering, programming, design). It wasn't a 'crisis' when outsourcing referred only to manufacturing. The outsourcing of professional and managerial labour (even the reading of CAT scans performed in the US or UK by Indian physicians) puts a lot of pressure on the (formerly) national frames of higher ed/cultural capitalism.

Equally important, as your great 'Free Labour' piece and Andrew Ross's 'The Mental Labour Problem' demonstrate, is the way that higher ed creates opportunities for hyper-exploitation.[1] Don't you think that higher ed is a primary vector for the harnessing of affect, socialising bodies to the necessary technologies and creating the psychological desire to give mental/affective labour away for less than a wage?

TT: Well, this would be consistent with Louis Althusser's notion of education as an 'Institutional State Apparatus' wouldn't it? And there is no doubt, as Foucault once put it, that the university still partially 'stands for the institutional apparatus through which society ensures its uneventful reproduction at the least cost to itself'. Sadie Plant used this quote to contest what she thinks is the 'Platonic' bias of many pedagogical approaches to higher education which contribute to making the university what Foucault said it was: the idea that knowledge is something that is 'recalled', ready made from an original source, and then simply transmitted from mind to mind. This is really the uneventful reproduction of readymade knowledges for the purposes of social reproduction.[2]

There is no doubt, that is, that the university is a site of reproduction of social knowledge and class stratifications. The range of courses and degrees now offered by higher education institutions means that today the university is producing nurses and doctors; managers and IT technicians; journalists, scientists, filmmakers, lawyers, artists, teachers and even waiters and the unemployed (yes, a degree does not always guarantee a 'middle class' job).

On the other hand, it is not simply reproducing classes and professions, but also participating in a larger process of qualitative recomposition at a moment of crisis for post-Fordism in the mode of information of which the outsourcing of white collar work from the US is an example. Higher ed is not simply engaged in the production and reproduction of knowledges, but also in that of an abstract social labour power, which can be multiply deployed across a range of productive sites (from call centres to Reality TV shows).

MB: Right.

TT: For me a key moment of this process involves an engagement with managerial control. I would like to talk about your essay on managerialism in 'rhet-comp' [rhetoric and composition].[3]

MB: That piece just observes that the informationalising or perma-temping of academic labour is not a neutral condition with respect to the knowledge that the academy produces. We call this the problem of 'Tenured Bosses and Disposable Teachers.'

In rhet-comp, which is a subfield of English language studies, traditionally lower in status than literature and linguistics, more than 90 percent of the teaching is done by flex workers. (Flex workers deliver labour 'in the mode of information,' as if they were data on the management desktop – easily called up by a keystroke, and then just as easily dropped in the trash.) Tenure is primarily reserved for persons who directly manage the temp workers, or who creatively theorise the work of supervised teaching. To a very real extent, the knowledge produced by the field is a knowledge for managers. Of course, not all the knowledge is about the work of management. Much of it is. But I think you could argue that even the field's knowledges on 'other questions' increasingly show the taint of the managerial world-view. There would have to be more research into that.

TT: So the tendency is for a collapse of the academic and managerial function in the service of institutional and social reproduction?

MB: Yes, but the real change is that it's more than just reproduction. Academic managerialism is increasingly in the direct service of extracting surplus value from students as well as staff. The university is an accumulation machine. It employs students directly and it farms cheap or donated student labour out to its 'corporate partners.'

The university's extraction of surplus value needs to be seen as an under-regulated 'semi-formal' economy. For-profit universities accumulate investment capital. But 'non-profit' universities also accumulate in the form of buildings, grounds, libraries (fixed capital), and as investment capital in endowments. Accumulated resources, such as campus sports facilities have to be understood, to a degree, as the collective property of the ruling class (as opposed to, say, the property of students). For instance, at my public research university, few students can afford to go to basketball games – local elites occupy all the seats.

As has been suggested elsewhere, especially by the players themselves, student athletes are unpaid workers contributing to campus and corporate accumulation.

TT: What seems to be at stake, then, is not simply the reproduction of a dominant ideology, but also more explicitly the attempt to induce and/or capture (and contain and control) a biopolitical surplus value that exceeds social reproduction, a potential to induce social transformations and produce new forms of life.

What I am saying is that even if many graduates are going to be disillusioned with the actual earnings and working conditions (or lack of) that they will have to face, it is difficult to know what this outsourced and redundant surplus of educated labour could turn into – how it is going to interact with the communication machine, for example. I think that the early phase of the 'free labour' bonanza (where many chose to perform work that they perceived as rewarding either for free or for very little money) is over. At least in Europe, I have noticed a great interest in the problem of the exploitation (and economic sustainability) of autonomous, 'creative' labour.

MB: I wish there was a similar interest in the US. It's definitely a question within managerial discourse, but still far less so in the mass of 'creative' labour. There is, of course, the graduate employee union movement, but there's almost nothing in the undergraduate population. The primary form of undergraduate labour activism remains the anti-sweatshop movement. It's very encouraging, of course. But it has real limits. It's not an activism that proceeds from the situation of the student as labour, but from the situation of the student as consumer. The problem of the undergraduate as labour – as you say, an element of production – is almost completely unexplored. I have had two students write dissertations that partially speak to the topic. But there's really almost nothing on it. At least in the US, there's very little law and policy on the question as well. That's what I mean when I talk about the 'informal economy' of the informationalised university. The relations of production going on under the sign of 'student' or 'study' or 'youth' are desperately under-regulated. It's a question of hyper-exploitation.

There is a bit more work on the student as a future worker, especially as a mental labourer, but very little. It's not framed as a question of a reserve army, but rather as a question of 'extended youth,' which young people are represented as 'choosing.' It's really a version of the Puritan discourse, where your social and economic positioning is read as a function of your moral state. The under-employed (with 'slack time') are so, because they're morally slack, therefore require the benevolent intervention of work disciplines such as speed-up.

TT: Yes, the Protestant spirit is, at many levels, well and alive in managerial discourse. And maybe you have a point when you say that, from capital's viewpoint, it is simply a matter of building an informational reserve army of workers. On the other hand, we also need to ask what social needs and desires and what processes of subjectivation does this reserve army express – what values it is capable of creating.

The question is also that of a direct and active engagement with specific student populations and their relation to this socialised labour power at large. This is why I have problems with a common counter-hegemonic argument against tuition fees (the hegemonic arguments being that 'we cannot afford mass higher education' or the 'many should not pay for the few' and that 'a degree is a financial investment for the future'). The counter-hegemonic argument, by contrast, says that by making financial costs between different institutions variable, poorer students are kept away from the 'best' institutions. The argument is that tuition fees make social mobility across classes more difficult.

All of this is true, of course, but I think that it only captures a fraction of the huge depletion of resources that is thus perpetrated at the expense of a mass intellectuality. By making tuition fees variable, as you know well from the US, you also automatically make working conditions (and pay usually follows) dramatically different across different layers and sections of academic labour.

MB: You want to get beyond the liberal complaint about social mobility. It's a more fundamental question of equality?

TT: In a way. In another way, this notion of equality still identifies knowledge too much with access to a limited cultural capital – rather than the huge, diverse and mutating flux of specialised knowledges and transversal connections which is a trademark of social production in network societies. It is not only a matter that the best lecturers will tend to flow towards the institutions where working conditions are better (less students and admin; more money for research; access to international academic networks, etc.). It is mainly about how a large part of the living labour within the higher education system will be impeded by higher workloads, scarce resources and tighter managerial control from actively engaging and experimenting with the massification of socialised labour power. Such power does not express itself simply as a unified or even fragmented class, but also as a constellation of singularities connected by communication machines and informational dynamics. All of this at a moment when organised labour is lagging behind (or is being easily accommodated by) the huge transformations induced by post-Fordism and globalisation.

MB: Going back to the question you raised about the role of living knowledge labour in transformation. I completely agree with you that the biopolitical potential is there in the lived experience of the student.

Their experience, especially of frustrated expectations, leaves them 'primed' and potentially volatile in all the ways you describe. After all, the huge role the US professional and managerial fraction plays in organising production globally has thus far created an oversized managerial fraction relative to the size of the state. And the oversized role of the US – also Europe and Japan of course – in world consumption is related to the expectations associated with the labour of managing globally.

So the frustration of those outsized expectations is volatile in ways we totally haven't explored. And yet there is, at the same time, a proportionately greater effort devoted to containing it.

TT: It's hard to know where it might go.

MB: The question of tuition brings me back to what you said before about the socialising function of education debt – about students being schooled by indebtedness. That is such an immense field for future research. Randy Martin has written about it in *The Financialisation of Daily Life*, in a great chapter about the politics of debt.[4] Debt is a way of making the relationship to dead labour more intimate than any possible relationship to living labour.

TT: Yes.

MB: There's something to be said about schooling, especially the university, and the whole system of cultural capitalism and shaping the relationship of living labour to dead labour. It would be great to think in more detail what it means to understand 'cultural capital' as dead labour.

Anyway, what I really like about the questions you're posing is the way it insists that we return to the question of the relationship of mental labour to other forms of labour. Are knowledge workers a 'class' unto themselves? Or are they a class fraction? If the latter, are they à la Bourdieu, the 'dominated fraction of the dominant class'? Or à la Gramsci, are they the fraction of the working class that tends toward a traitorous alliance with the ruling class?

I tend to think that your work confirms the Gramscian position. I suppose that follows necessarily from the autonomist point of view.

TT: This is a really interesting question. Gramsci was a keen observer of 'civil society' – and he was very aware that the complex relation between social classes was a historical and dynamic relation of shifting alliances, with hegemony constituting a kind of 'moving equilibrium'. The space of civil society, however, is relatively solid, stratified and bounded. Classes enter relationships of alliance, but are clearly distinguishable within the overall boundary of the nation state and the dialectic opposition between the dominant and the dominated.

MB: But for you it's more a question of reinventing the terms of the struggle itself.

TT: Autonomist work started with trade union sponsored social research into the reasons for declining union membership. The result of that theoretical, empirical and political inquiry was a foregrounding of the alchemical dynamics of class composition. Union membership was declining, because neither the structure of the union nor its culture could cope with a shifting class composition (such as an increasing number of young, male, unskilled immigrant workers and their refusal of the unionist work ethic). This was not simply a new contingent coming to join the old generation, but also implied a new set of social needs and desires, which not only the union, but factory work as such, could not satisfy. The figure of this first transformation was the 'mass worker' – unskilled, mass factory work that challenged the industrial production machine through the rigidity of its escalating demands and its simultaneous social mobility. The mass worker demanded and caused a reinvention of politics, rather than simply joining the class struggle as a new contingent would – it gave new impetus to the struggle for life time against the 'time-measure' of the wage/work relation. An implication is that class is not simply about the reproduction of dialectical domination, but it is also endowed with its own historicity – a kind of dynamic potential, a surplus of value that antagonistically produces new forms of life and demands new modes of political and cultural expression.

Which brings us to today's question. Should we read the expansion of higher education as, primarily, a desire of capital (for better trained, more manageable, stratified and hegemonised workers)? Or should we read in this transformation also the recomposition of class dynamics – a new production of values and forms of life which produce the basis for the reinvention of politics?

MB: Would it be waffling of me to say both are true? Just as the university is industrialised (albeit on a post-Fordist footing of perma-temped labour in the mode of information), it – like the factory – becomes the location of an oppositional agency. Students – in their new character as workers in the present rather than the future – will, in my view, eventually understand themselves as the agents of their own exploitation. At that moment, we'll understand the information university to have called forth its own gravediggers.

TT: Sure. And as usual, we must be careful about not repeating the old mistake of thinking of the working class as existing in a state of 'unrealised consciousness', which needs to be awoken by an external agency. If we keep this in mind, the main question becomes then not so much to map different fractions of the dominant and dominated classes and their relation to each other within the overall war of position, but to understand the shifting mode of class composition, its dynamics and the values that it produces (taking into account, for example, the heterogeneous axes of subjectivation linked to ethnicity, race, nationality, gender, sexuality and so on). The shift from the 'mass worker' to 'socialised labour power' (or a multi-skilled, fully socialised and abstract labour power), was for the early Negri a matter of achieving a new working class identity – one that was adequate to the increasing levels of abstraction and socialisation of labour. The old transcendent dialectic was replaced with an immanent one: class composition, capitalist restructuration, class recomposition.[5] In other authors, such as Franco

Berardi or Felix Guattari, however, the break with the dialectic is more radical. The emphasis is more on the heterogeneous production of subjectivity, which takes place at the level of material connections (crucially including desiring and technical machines, from the assembly line to media and computer networks).

Subjectivity and class are not simply modes of reproduction, but also alchemical, microbiological and machinic factories of social transformation.

MB: I agree.

TT: We could maybe close by talking about the place of academic labour within the labour movement at large (including all those mutant forms of labour that the trade union movement cannot reach).

MB: The one thing I would say is that it couldn't be a privileged place. To give academic labour a vanguard position would be a disaster. A big part of the academic 'labour of reproduction' is the production, legitimation and policing of inequality. I think academic labour, including organised academic labour, needs to submit itself to the tutelage of more radical forms of labour self-organisation. More radical than the trade union movement, as you say. Mass intellectuality implies a revolutionary transformation in the academic consciousness, faculty especially.

That's why I place so much emphasis on thinking about students as already workers, not just future workers. They are less ossified, less committed to inequality, than the faculty. To a certain extent, they are also not invested in the labor aristocracy/bureaucracy of the trade unions. It would be crazy to call student life the perfect crucible for a movement to create greater equality. But the massification of higher ed has made it more likely. This is not nostalgia for 1968. Far from it. I think that the gigantic expansion of student experience, to the point where we have to see it as a modality of worker experience, creates opportunities so much larger than '68.

TT: I don't know about 'tutelage', but I would definitely be for a greater effort to open up connections with other forms of labor on the basis of what academic labor shares with them (from the common plague of managerial command and its attack on the time of life to the common implication in the diffuse social factory). On the other hand, there is also a specific contribution that academic labor can provide. This specificity is part of its role as a key site in the production and reproduction of knowledges and forms of control (from policy-oriented social research to scientific patents and new technologies); in its contribution to the production of specific forms of labor directly implicated in the reproduction of the social (from doctors to computer scientists, from managers to artists and social workers); but also in its relation to a wider abstract social labour power (informated, affective and communicational), which exceeds the disciplinary power of the work/wage relation. As you said, a big part of the university's work is still institutional: reproducing hierarchical differences and producing docile subjects, so hacking the machine of social reproduction in higher ed is bound to be complicated work. I doubt whether a successful engagement with this process would produce another 1968 – the latter was still a revolt against the institutions, while we know now that power operates in and through networks. But it will definitely be a challenging process to be part of – requiring commitment and imagination.

Footnotes:

[1] Tiziana Terranova, "Free Labour: Producing Culture for the Digital Economy" and Andrew Ross, 'The Mental Labour Problem', both in *Social Text 63*, Vol.18, No.2: Summer 2000

[2] Sadie Plant "The Virtual Complexity of Culture" in G. Robertson et al (eds) *FutureNatural: nature/science/culture*. London: Routledge, 1996

[3] Marc Bousquet, Tony Scott, Leo Parascondola, eds. *Tenured Bosses and Disposable Teachers: Writing Work in the Managed University*, Southern Illinois, 2004

[4] Randy Martin, *The Financialisation of Daily Life*, Philadelphia: Temple UP, 2002

[5] Antonio Negri "Archaeology and Project: The Mass Worker and the Social Worker" in *Revolution Retrieved: Selected Writings on Marx, Keynes, Capitalist Crisis & New Social Subjects 1967-83*. London: Red Notes, 198

Previously published in: *Mute Magazine*, Issue 28, Summer-Autumn, 2004; also available at: http://www.metamute.org/en/Recomposing-the-University

Intro taken from the aforementioned issue of *Mute Magazine*.

The Continual Crisis of Capitalism

An Interview with John Barker
17.08.2008

Author of the book Bending the bars *and regular contributor to* Variant *and* Mute *magazines, John Barker has been involved with a wide range of anti-capitalist, organised labour struggles since the late 1960s. Tapping into this 40-year engagement and struggle with the many contradictions of capitalism, he helps us understand the intricacies and likely outcomes of the current manifestation of the crisis, the central role of structural greed and the vulnerability of neoliberalism in the face of myriad forms of disobedience and defiance.*

(RK) Rosa Kerosene
(JB) John Barker

RK: First of all John, welcome and thanks for giving up your time to enter into this telephone conference and email exchange. As you know, we are putting together a publication, the idea for which came about as a form of address to those educational institutions producing programmes and literature that promote the primacy of the market against a backdrop of increasing student hardship and indebtedness. For us, at least, the current crisis in capitalism should be factored into the debate on education and a basic grasp of what's going on 'outside', so to speak, would be of immense use. In fact, we'd like to go further and situate this debate inside the walls of the institution and launch a direct challenge to acquiescence with neoliberal agendas.

Crisis

RK: Capitalist crisis — can you have one without the other? It seems that no one really understands what is happening in the complex markets that have developed over the last few years. Thus, there is a large potential for power to be achieved by an individual or group who says they DO understand. Whether this is someone working within banking, a financial journalist, a critical artist, a left-wing author or even a group of people editing a journal. Do you think we can understand, first of all, what might be happening in this so-called credit crunch, and if we can't understand, how could we proceed?

JB: I have a problem immediately with the phrase 'capitalist crisis', for several reasons. I am sixty years old now and all my life there have been various capitalist crises. More importantly, life under capitalism is a permanent economic crisis for so many people in the world. So I am a little sceptical about exactly what we mean. The classic crisis – the one which we could say today concerns, in Marxist terms, the realisation of profit – is that if you're squeezing the wages of the people who produce, they, who are also consumers, will not have the income to consume what has been produced. Or Keynesians would call it a deficiency in 'effective demand'. And it involves, also in Marxist terms, the expansion of credit beyond what can be 'productively' used.

What is happening now has many of the same features as what went before, but that doesn't mean it is the same. There are many new factors which enable us in a direct political way, even if it's arguing the points with everybody we know, to talk loud and clear of two things.

One is the very simple slogan 'privatised profit, socialised risk', which has a lot of resonance. At a time when we have already entered recession, when house prices are falling rapidly, one could be thinking that, politically, there might be a lot of what I would call 'middle class resentment'. That resentment can, of course, go in very nasty directions. We have a job to do to keep hammering home that it is the normally sacred character of bourgeois politics, the taxpayer, who is in fact socialising the risk, while profit remains private.

The other thing, and I don't know what its implications are, is the crisis in the integrity of information. This has really come to the fore in a world of 'think tanks', 'think tank' reality and 'think tank' descriptions of the world, which have very little relation to reality. Where you have banks suing each other on the grounds that they were not told the full story about some package of derivatives that they have been sold, this crisis in the integrity of information is made visible. We've seen the way ratings agencies have been criticised. Obviously ratings agencies are paid by investment banks, so there is a conflict of interest. But they are also claiming that they don't have access to the full information, even though these are the very same people who ascribe how much credit it is going to cost different people in different parts of the world – which as we know, in previous periods has been terribly expensive for the people in Brazil, for example, and this only for political reasons. So I think one of the things that is really different is this crisis in the integrity of information.

RK: In terms of the media, and the information it provides, the economics team at the BBC has recently been shuffled and in some cases promoted, suggesting that the organisation wants top people in place to deal with what is the major ongoing news story. 'Depth and insight' were cited in press announcements about the appointments. Is the information traded by such news organisations intact? Can you

*elaborate further on this "crisis in the integrity of information" and the
role of the mainstream media?*

JB: When banks are suing other banks, or hedge funds are suing banks,
or banks are suing hedge funds, then it IS public. There is this very
important case being carried out in New York against top executives in
Bear Stearns, partly for insider trading. Insider trading is not new, but
they are also being accused of not giving out enough information, and
this is a criminal offence. I suspect this is because there is a worry in the
US, following the dot-com bubble, about that other sacred character of
bourgeois politics, one so well represented by, for example, the BBC: 'the
investor'. That he/she might be saying "I don't want to invest, because I
can't trust anything." The investors are freaking out. So now the
regulatory authorities are making an example of Bear Stearns. It's
terrible how this does not filter into the mainstream media. But then the
BBC has had neoliberalism as a default ideology for many years. That is
another job of ours, to confront it. On occasion, I get really angry, and
instead of shouting at the TV, I actually send an email complaining about
their coverage. What is particularly noticeable is that compared to 10
years ago, certainly to 20 years ago, these anchor people – who as you
said bring extra depth, etc. – are called in as neutral experts but they are
always from so and so asset research of Lombard Street or from Merrill
Lynch research department, and you almost never hear any voice from
trade unions. That really is a significant shift in the last few years. We are
talking about a crisis in the integrity of self-knowledge. The mainstream
media continues a monologue. In the past it has been capable of listening
to other voices, but at the moment it seems to be a monologue, and thus
surely amplifies the crisis of the integrity of information.

*RK: Can we briefly return to the question of a general crisis in
capitalism? You've listed points that make this current situation unique
– the 'privatisation of profit and the socialisation of risk' and the 'crisis
in the integrity of information'. Can you identify any parallels or
similarities with previous moments of capitalist crises?*

JB: Well, as I said earlier, the classic explanation of crises is the problem
with the realisation of profit, the disparity that is being made an
ideological reality, between the same person as consumer and exactly
the same person as producer. The Keynesian nexus whereby this
relationship worked in a relatively stable manner was broken so
decisively by neoliberalism. I remember, for example, soon after the East
Asia crisis and the collapse of the ironically named 'Long-Term Capital
Management' hedge fund, when the US Federal Reserve forced other
banks to rescue it (1998 – ed.), there was one of these 'wise guys' who
said "we need all the yuppies we can muster". He was saying that in order
to still actually realise profits, they would need such people. They were

obviously looking at the creation of a global consumer class in China, India and Brazil, which although only a small percentage of the populations of those countries, still means around 300 - 400 million people who now become global consumers. I think that capital has seen this as a way out of its problems. Massimo De Angelis is right in the other way it has worked. The actual decline of real wages in the US, for example, over the last ten years, has been masked by reversed prices, i.e. the cheapness of products made in Southeast Asia and consumed in the US. This crisis IS different, because the cheapness of East Asian products cannot compensate for serious increases in the price of food, gas and oil; the disguise of that decline in real wages has gone. People have to spend more of their income on these basic things.

Work

RK: Yes, but surely if the insecurities created by the decline in real wages, or the lifting of its disguise are in any way linked to the situation in emerging economies, then international worker solidarity becomes less possible?

JB: Sorry, but I do see it the other way. What has been pushed very hard by the bourgeois media in the direction of workers elsewhere in the world is: "the Chinese are coming" – so be careful about making any demands or capital will simply shift there. In a way, it's been used to terrorise the working class of the Western World. This has been posed as if there was no class struggle in China. But there is class struggle in China, there are more strikes and protests there than anywhere else in the world. If you look back at the way the bourgeoisie really got freaked out by the demonstrations in Seattle against the World Trade Organisation, for instance, there were environmentalists, anti-capitalists and there were these "reactionary" American workers, as the media would have it, who were anxious about their jobs. Politically it was a brilliant coalition and it is the maintenance of that coalition that is important. In fact, the push-up for wages in the Western World would help Chinese workers push up for their wages. It has at times been argued by some 'Third World leaders' that they didn't want to have health and safety standards for their workers, that the attempt to impose them was a form of imperialism, because if they were imposed those countries couldn't compete with the Western World. But this underestimates the real class struggle that is going on in China, in Brazil and increasingly in India. About 25 years ago, there was an organisation called the 'Ford Workers combine', which was completely 'grass roots' – outside of any trade union bureaucracy. This 'Ford Workers combine' managed to hold international meetings between Ford workers from all over the world. This seems to me to be an absolute model, and I wish they would write this up. In the development of the Dockers strike in Liverpool, you could see these links being made. Dockers went to America and Australia and got support in various 'wildcat' actions. They used the internet. They did finally lose, but the strike was about discipline, the power for management to discipline them in a way that they would have to work much harder for the same money. But it was also about their power to manage, their power to discipline. This had a resonance with dock workers in many parts of the world. I do think that the union movement is wising up. We used to say that union leaders were all sell-out bastards, but I think they are actually being pushed to wise up and start thinking in terms of global alliances. Either, as in the case of the Ford Combine, within a particular company, or within a certain sector, such as the global meeting of militant workers in the chemical industry, for instance. That is where I see a possibility. Also, this process of wising-up is taking place in the wider movement for radical social change. In the past, the environmental movement (I do not include here the use of 'environmentalism' to dispossess the poor) has often been seen as Malthusian, i.e. that it has been used by capitalism to talk of limits only when it has suited them to talk of limits, which invariably are limits on consumption by those who one way or another produce surplus value. Many activists see the necessity for a class aware green politics. This wising-up has been manifested in various social forums, some more successfully than others. There are problems, of course, we can't hold the World Social Forum up as an absolute, we can't fetishise it, but what we can see in Latin America is how what we call grass roots politics has actually worked and developed and had an influence over institutional politics.

Trade unions

RK: In "Intensities of Labour"[1] you state that "Everybody working for a wage should be in a trade union." We were comparing that to the idea that trade unions can only achieve the 'normal' grade of exploitation, but nothing more. Maybe you could expand on the potential you see in trade unions.

JB: The fact that unions are not going to change the world, that they are not going to make a revolution tomorrow, is not the relevant point. It's particularly not the relevant point now. The most interesting union organising that is going on in this country is amongst low-paid workers. They are making active efforts to unionise, particularly in the food processing industry, where work has been under the most exploitative conditions. Unions are beginning to suss out how to operate against this. Usually, large capital like the supermarkets hide behind a chain of sub-contractors and say what the sub-contractor does is not our responsibility, as if "our hands are clean". But increasingly unions are pushing and shaming large capitalist organisations, with their 'goody-goody' PR. The food industry employs around 400,000 people, many of whom have the most terrible health and safety conditions, for example, those working in cold storage are cold all the time. So it's really important that you fight for very basic things such as having a regular 10 minute break in order to come out of cold storage. It's only trade unions that can negotiate these kinds of real things. They made a conscious decision, certainly among the Transport and General Workers, to recruit and agitate on chains of production in the food industry. They will say "where the weak link is", and the weak link might be Sainsbury's, who present themselves as a very ethical supermarket, so you start embarrassing them. They have been very slow to pick up on things, but I think that they are doing it now. Some of the people involved in the Liverpool Dock strike who are now unemployed have set up a group both to analyse the composition of catering work in Liverpool and to inform, and possibly form, unions. What they found, is that the crucial element in the catering industry in Liverpool is in fact students, as they are relatively cheap labour, expendable or without contracts and so on. This process of examining what the Italian Autonomists called 'class composition' is not intended as an aesthetic analysis, but to have real consequences in organising. What trade unions are wising up to is not exactly the same, but involves the analysis of chains of production, and looking for organising possibilities and weak points. I am not trying to fetishise trade unions, however, but talking about organisation in places where you work, and unions have been the traditional way that this has been done. If they can be motivated to support struggles in a particular area, say in the culture industries, then unions are useful. So, I do believe, yes, that everybody working for a wage should be in a trade union, wherever possible. Obviously, it is difficult in the kind of work you're presumably going into, where people are on short-term contracts and so on, but again, I think unions have become practically involved in 'precarity' struggles and are increasingly interested in how conditions can be improved, even within temporary contracts and part-time work. It is here that I have a problem with the Bolshevik view point that this type of union activity is 'merely' reformism or 'economism'. Especially in the present, where neoliberalism finds any resistance to what it says 'the market' demands intolerable.

It's not just that they don't have union people in the mass media, it's that they freak out at even very small union struggles – they think that this is going to undermine – and this for me is always the crucial political question – the social discipline which is manifested through capitalism. These things may look like very small struggles about very small things, but they have a political relevance and impact. Neoliberalism has a very thin skin, it can't take much – it freaks out! It can't take it.

Structural greed

RK: In your most recent text "Structural Greed: The Credit Crunch"[2] you take a fairly distinctive position on the current 'credit crisis', positing the concept of 'structural greed' as the main underlying element of global capitalism, the consequences of which – increased intensities of labour, decreases in real wages and rising costs of basic living materials – people are feeling globally to different extremes. In terms of doing the "job of contesting capitalism's own account of its own present crisis", to quote from the text, it seems that a general acceptance and understanding of structural greed would be central to that. So, what is it exactly?

JB: The notion of greed is a moral concept. In post-Marx Marxism, the moral content has always been underplayed, because of the pretensions of Marxism to be science and to be scientific, which was obviously a 19th century pressure. Marx himself is both a moralist and an analyst of how capital works, providing a materialist understanding of what's going on. So, for example, in the Highland Clearances[3] or on the Paris Commune, you read a passionate morality and then he also gives you a penetrating analysis of how 19th century capitalism actually works. So he's doing the two things. However, I think that greed as a moral notion has disappeared from the presentation of the world by 'Marxists'. Though ironically, even the Governor of the Bank of England used the word greed a couple of months ago, complaining about graduates who should have been in physics laboratories, but were in fact earning huge amounts of money, manipulating financial packages.

All this is true when so many conflicts of interest have now been revealed to be the norm, but I wanted also to get at the role of 'the investor', and how it has become a privileged category. A lot of people have written about securitization, the role of credit, what credit does, etc. But I was concerned with the way in which finance capital might be isolated as the source of all evil, which politically can easily be called Jewish capital, or cosmopolitan capital, too. This is something that has actually happened in the past. So I wanted to get at the role of the investor in two ways. One was to challenge the notion that industrial capital is somehow morally superior to finance capital. Should we talk about companies who produce armaments as morally superior, all those arms companies supported by the sacred taxpayer? You know, the biggest British manufacturing export is armaments. Is that morally superior? No, so I wanted to deal with that, but also to go back to the way in which this privileged category called the investor had been led, either by buying houses to rent, or by investing in hedge funds, or by investing in the stock market in Latin America where profits could be huge. And this privileged investor is looking for the highest rates of return, much higher than rates of return on, say, government bonds. We're talking about 8-10 times bigger. All of which were claims on surplus value, claims for a larger share. But the global pot of surplus value is always limited at any given moment. At the same time, even though these things were supposed to be risky, the investor was constantly being cocooned from the consequences of risk. Which is why this slogan 'privatised profit – socialised risk' is one that is very uniting at the present time. Pension funds, for example, are used as an alibi for the greed of the investor, or the assumption that the investor is entitled to these massive rates of return. Pension funds are used as if we were all complicit in this, as if we would all benefit, even though a lot of the funds have lost out.

I felt it was very important that the MAI, the Multi-Lateral Agreement on Investment, was actually successfully resisted, because this would have given investors the right to sue national governments if they didn't do exactly what was suitable to capital. Although, unfortunately, this is happening in a lot of trade deals from bilateral, Western countries with individual, less developed countries. I think they're getting these kinds of concessions for the rights of international investors.

So that's what I meant by structural greed. That it was both individuals getting paid £10 million pounds and getting these incredible bonuses, which obviously were a contributing factor to them wanting to sell dodgy mortgages. This happened; personal greed is real. But I also felt that it was more remote and that people who have no direct relationship to the effects of production and exploitation had been led to expect that they could go on having high rates of return.

RK: Would you say that putting forward structural greed in place of 'credit crunch' or perhaps even capitalism, changes the idea of struggle in some way? Is there a shift in focus, or a more intense focus, on what's really at the base of everything?

JB: There are people who are teachers and doctors, the professional middle class, who are pissed off when they see people taking huge bonuses even when they've fucked up, even when they've actually made a mistake in their risk management. And as I say, I do think that that's important, because the other possibility is of a certain middle class resentment turning against the weakest positions, migrant workers, for example. If there is a serious recession, as is possible or likely, house prices, instead of being this thing that you can guarantee making you richer by the year will actually drop in value massively. I think this will make people resentful. It's going to make them angry and their anger could be directed in many different ways. We know the mass media will endeavour to direct that resentment towards people who are poorer and in a weaker position than they are. Our job is obviously to direct this anger to the really powerful people who have in fact benefited, and are still making their bonuses, despite the recession that's going to hit the rest of us. This might be seen as populist politics, but I don't see that as a problem if it becomes popular to say: look at these greedy bastards. And also to make 'privatised profit – socialised risk' a popular slogan, because the risk here involves another category. It is not just the investor who is a good guy, we've also got the taxpayer (in fact we are all taxpayers), who is also usually presented as a good guy of the middle class being taken advantage of by uppity public sector workers. In this instance, however, he or she is being taken advantage of by the rescue of banks, particularly the rescue of Northern Rock in which the assurances that the taxpayer will get all their money back are not, I think, worth very much. The middle class is a very general, and probably increasingly useless term, because it comprises so many people with in fact different sets of interests and different relationships to the chain of exploitation. Most importantly, we can see the proletarianisation of forms of labour which were previously considered to be middle class or career structured or privileged in some way. I think they are the people who may form a solid political block against the possible resentment directed at migrant labour or other easy targets. The work of – I dare to use the word 'us' – all of us who believe that capitalism is an inherently unhealthy, killing system should be to focus on systematic greed, in clear opposition to blame directed at migrant labour or, on the other hand, 'Jewish' finance capital.

Immaterial labour

RK: In relation to this widening of the struggle among different classes, and the potential for that struggle to turn against itself (for example in the form of racist or nationalist propaganda), we've been discussing what we consider to be effective critiques of concepts linked to the Multitude, and Autonomia, for instance the critique of immaterial labour in David Graeber's "The Sadness of Post Workerism". We would be very curious to hear your take on his critique of the Negri, Lazzarato circus that hit the Tate Gallery.

JB: I thought it was a very good piece, but should say straight away that certainly in the 1970s Negri was very important to me. I think he was incredibly astute, and I'd like to come back to what he was astute about. In terms of what I said before about unions and class struggle at the point of production, the Italian Autonomy movement in the 1970s and into the 1980s was important precisely in posing an alternative to that Bolshevism obsessed only with the limits of labour struggles. Comrades like Sergio Bologna and Ferrucio Gambino, who were all from the same tradition as Negri, are still doing really important work, in which their theoretical considerations are grounded in serious research work into the realities of global capital, labour process and the role of the price of oil. Graeber's probably right in the end that Negri himself, as he describes very well, now speaks like a prophet. He's been through a lot, exile and imprisonment, which most leftists haven't, but I can't say whether prophet is a necessary, important or justifiable role.

The notion of immaterial labour has been kicked to death from all sorts of directions. There's a fabulous piece in *Mute* by Brian Ashton,[4] who was actually from the Liverpool Dockers campaign, about the global logistics industry, in which the notion of immaterial labour as against the notion of material labour just becomes nonsense, because in worldwide logistics these two forms of work are totally integrated. One of the three or four important books I've read in my life is Harry Braverman's *Labour and Monopoly Capital* in which, even in the 1970s, he was particularly good on the actual details of de-skilling and the relationship between the way in which material labour processes were being modified solely in the interests of increasing the intensity of labour. But I do think the notion of immaterial labour has been rendered pretty useless, and in fact, a diversion.

RK: To shortly go back to your position on unions. There seems to have been a major shift in your viewpoint over the last 40 years, from organisations willing to sell out their members, to an effective way of organising against capital. What was your position then and how has it changed?

JB: We used to go on demonstrations denouncing union leaderships as sell-outs, which they frequently were. They were in a position of strength, which they didn't fully take advantage of and they made lots of unnecessary compromises, because in fact they shared a lot of values with government. Negri in the 1970s had been incredibly prescient. What he was prescient about in writing around 1973 and 1974, this crucial point in modern capitalist history, was that after a period where politics in general, and particularly the labour movement, were used to a situation where negotiations could be made with governments or employers federations, he said we are now entering a situation where there will be nobody to negotiate with. As I understand it now, what happened at this time – and I think this is really important – is the reason why, even though I don't want to isolate finance capital as the source of all evils, I still believe that because of measures taken by politicians, finance capital actually became the way to discipline workers around the world, because industrial capital had realised that working class struggle was winning too many gains, particularly in the late 1960s and early 1970s and particularly in Italy. A combination of petrodollars, the political decision to make currencies 'floating', and then the further political decisions to liberalise movement of capital, meant that market confidence/sentiment became the determining factor in so much political and economic struggle. This was even before "the Chinese are coming". "Market confidence" is itself determined by the balance of class forces and level of social discipline in any one country so that the investor class and its representatives could punish places which they did not approve of by "investment strikes" or by the undermining of currencies. It has taken a while – too long – but progressive governments, and now trade unions, are beginning to adjust to a situation where there is no one to negotiate with by searching out those weak points which might, and do allow for negotiation, which neoliberalism is wholly hostile to, since negotiations are invariably a can of worms where notions of fairness and justice are always likely to appear. This seems especially possible when the untouchable sanctity of "the market" has been undermined by the holes revealed in finance capital.

I should just qualify this in that I've used the union movement as a short hand. What I'm really talking about is how important fighting over wages, conditions, health and safety at work is, about how politically important that is, and unions happen to have been the form through which most of this has taken place. I'm not in any way trying to idealise trade unions. A lot of their leaderships are very New Labour, accepting the realities of neoliberalism, but increasingly even the leaderships are now being pushed by the demands of neoliberalism in terms of de-skilling, privatisation, increasing intensity of labour, and so on and so forth. Even union leaderships are being pushed to develop ways in which they can reestablish their membership numbers, and also be recruiting in areas which were new to their traditional industrial workplaces. I think there is anecdotal evidence that this is the case, but as I said I wasn't trying to fetishise trade unions, but simply to talk about the importance of struggles at work.

De-skilling

RK: In "Intensities of Labour" you mention de-skilling as a means of reducing the economic and political potential of workers by replacing skilled labour with fixed capital or machines. What seems interesting in relation is to posit the university as a site of both de-skilling, e.g. teachers replaced by learning software; and also re-skilling, e.g. the de-skilled labour force constantly needing to acquire new skills. We are interested in the roles de-skilling and re-skilling play in the reduction of space and time, as well as in the potential for critical thought and resistance within the university, in terms of its impact on the political potential of student movements, and also how that impacts upon the labour market.

JB: Well, there is technological development and there is technological development. That happens on two levels, one is what is invested in; why are armaments invested in? Why has, for example, the male contraceptive pill, which has been talked about for 20 years, not got anywhere? So there's a question of what's invested in what. We know the way modernisation covers a multitude of sins. There are obviously technologies and technologies, and workers have had to assess which technical processes in production are possibly beneficial to them and which are more than likely going to increase what I call the intensity of labour, which might mean having to concentrate or be 'focused' all the time, for 8 hours a day on a particular process, whereas before you could do it almost automatically without thinking. Not that that is a virtue. I quoted Milan Kundera in the article, saying that a lot of Czech dissidents had taken the simplest factory jobs, because then it wouldn't involve them having to give any of their brains to the process. Intensity of labour has been the speed-up of processes, more concentration, and in the article I drew attention to a new form especially at work in cultural industries, which is the demand that you believe your work, however banal its product, to be really important. In addition, precarity and the capitalist domination of technological development demands a constant learning process and the anxiety that one might be left behind. This is, not to say that such jobs are not relatively privileged, despite the proletarianisation of many students and teachers. The statistics in America do show that graduates are likely to earn X number of times more income than people without degrees over their lifetimes. But again, I don't think you can worry about that. If people in the cultural industries accept new rounds of exploitation, this is not of itself going to help workers in conditions of even greater exploitation. That is a lie of bourgeois ideology. The fight within the world of the university to keep the notion of critical thinking as the object of education is crucial. In elite universities, where the next generation of the elite is trained, critical thinking is allowed, but this would appear to not be the case in a lot of educational institutions where education is far more instrumental and functional to what they believe creative capital, or whatever you want to call it, is going to require. This ironically is also undermined, for example, by the very high levels of rent in London, which actually mean that it's very difficult for young people, whose parents don't have money, to become part of that creative industries class.

The thinness of neoliberal skin

RK: In your text "The Angry Brigade"[5] you state that "These days all campaigns of the oppressed which might once have been called reformist are close to the knuckle, bread and butter strikes and almost automatically a challenge to the ruling fetish of managerial authority."

Your argumentation seems to be that minor fights are very important at the moment and have a bigger impact than they would have had in earlier days.

JB: Well I think that's a very fair summary of what I was saying. I'd like to put this within the context of what I believe politics is about. That when we say we are anti-capitalist, we see that capitalism is a mode of exploitation which has an absolute necessity to accumulate profit, and accumulate more capital and is, in symbiotic fashion, a mode of social discipline. There are many different forms of discipline. One is managerial discipline and the fetish of managerialism, which is coming back a little bit, as well as that of the whiz kids of finance, who've been somewhat discredited, and I think in that we may get a resurgence of the notion of managerial expertise. But I do think that despite these different forms, neoliberalism is a monologue, and as Guy Debord wrote famously in "The Society of the Spectacle", monologues are more fragile than the diffuse power of what he called the spectacle. I think this level of monologue, as we see for instance in the challenge to the legitimacy of this kind of capitalism in Latin America, is very thin. It's thin-skinned and its sources of legitimacy are totally dependent on it coming up with at least enough goods to satisfy a politically powerful enough section of various populations in the world to stay in power. I think that that makes this legitimacy thin as does its monologue and that therefore challenges to its many many forms of discipline are all potentially very subversive.

RK: Just to come back to your comments on critical thinking. When we see institutions enthusiastically sponsoring critical studies and criticality, elite or not, it seems there is a tendency for subsumption, or even perhaps a method of control being inserted into institutionalised critique.

JB: Critical thinking should be encouraged everywhere, and I think it can only lead in one direction. If you really are encouraged to question most things, then I think you are going to become an anti-capitalist without too much difficulty. That is to say, if your critical intelligence is not stuck within parameters. In the age of the tyranny of opinion – and as the thinkers of the Scottish Enlightenment understood – I think it is absolutely necessary now to be part of working for a mass critical intelligence, and I think it is our duty, wherever we are, to encourage questions, and take nothing at face value.

Footnotes:

[1] John Barker, "Intensities of Labour: From Amphetamine to Cocaine", *Mute Magazine*, 07/03/2006, http://www.metamute.org/en/Intensities-of-Labour-from-Amphetamine-to-Cocaine

[2] John Barker, "Structural Greed: The Credit Crunch", *Variant Magazine*, Issue 32, Summer 2008, http://www.variant.randomstate.org/32texts/barker32.html

[3] Karl Marx, "The Duchess of Sutherland and Slavery", *The People's Paper*, No. 45, March 12 1853, http://www.marx.org/archive/marx/works/1853/03/12.htm

[4] Brian Ashton, "The Factory Without Walls", *Mute Magazine*, Volume II Issue 4, Winter 2007, http://www.metamute.org/en/Factory-Without-Walls

[5] John Barker, "The Angry Brigade", *Transgressions: A Journal of Urban Exploration*, Spring 1998, http://www.geocities.com/pract_history/barker.html

Struggle

Emancipatory Self-Organisation
and the Potential of Eruptions

The following text is derived from a conversation between Johannes Raether and Rosa Kerosene in summer 2008. It's about corporate critique and self-organisation in relation to the project My Academy, founded in 2004 at the opening of the Volkswagen Library of the Technical University and the Universität der Künste (UdK) in Berlin. My Academy took this as an opportunity to adopt the identities of Volkswagen workers in order to bring informative material about the background of the sponsoring deal to public attention.

My Academy was a very concrete project that arose at the junction of a particular contemporary crystallisation of political economy, education and institution. The background to My Academy is a classical form of self-organisation within the art academy. At a certain point, we decided that we wanted to define our studies at the Academy ourselves, and that it was up to us to put pressure on the usual hierarchies and flows of information that otherwise form inside the master class system, by creating them ourselves in self-organised groups thereby making them something possible to discuss. We didn't just want to determine our own content, as is probably the case in any more progressive kind of master class, but on the contrary to actually work collectively. Within this, we tried to develop criteria for how self-organisation could look today. Since the drastic reforms in the academies in the 1990s, and the fact that something like political art really is taught within academies now, we asked ourselves what would actually change if we were to do this ourselves; if we self-organise, but ultimately talk about the same content. We are not exactly going to reinvent leftist discourse just because we're self-organised, but we did try to define that differently through our structure. In the form in which My Academy manifested itself, it was not stringently clear how we were organised, but the project grew out of self-organised structures and also returned to self-organised structures. We worked together with various people in Berlin who were working in self-organised educational structures at that time. It is possible to organise yourself in a different way to that prescribed by the academy, and nevertheless to take on the academy. With My Academy, but above all with the Free Class, we repeatedly operated alongside this productive contradiction.

My Academy was therefore the attempt to extend everything that we had worked on in the context of the UdK in terms of organisation, structure and content – a very concrete critique of that specific institution – and to investigate the broader political connections that we currently perceive within higher education reform. We looked for models that could, figuratively, experientially and visibly map these developments out for us. The opening of the Volkswagen Library presented a good opportunity to deal with these different levels of neoliberal reform within higher education. It was for that reason that we founded My Academy along with other groups, as a type of alliance, and continued with it for over two years.

Corporate critique

How does one understand capitalism as political economy, and how does one develop a practice in relation to that? In the critique of corporations, or the critique of the sphere of circulation as pure speculation, a confrontation often emerges between so-called exploitative and productive capital. This often accompanies a discussion about the leeching American investment firms that are invading Europe and sucking the good German businesses dry, to subsequently sell them off at a profit.

What is the critique of capitalism if it remains suspended in the sphere of circulation? What is the critique of capitalism if it pits national, productive capital against the abstract American kind (or whoever else one suspects of being the current rogue nation)? One opens up a dichotomy between two forms of capital that actually represent a specific ideology, an ideology that masks the abstract way in which capitalism actually works.

It was very important for us to reflect, in the form of our critique, the various questions and observations that we had seen in the critique of capitalism.

We had developed a significant uneasiness towards the connect-ability of our critique – among right as well as left-wing professors at the university; we could discern there fronts forming at cross-purposes to one another. It was obvious that almost everyone applauds you when you start bashing a corporation. But our critique wasn't meant to be seen as a critique of the corporation as a kind of personal character. It was rather directed at the corporation as a representative in its relationship with a state protagonist that in common and mutual agreement and exertion of influence, dissolves a particular connection that had established itself under the welfare state, and that we, at least in part, considered to be worth maintaining.

Self-organization

What's also important is to critically question the form of self-organisation that was developed in the 1970s, which we simply appropriate today as something positive, as a 'fighting term' to be deployed at the front against antiquated and encrusted structures. What can self-organisation be today? One could say, in this phase of advanced capitalism, that the term cannot be used without an adjective anymore and can be specified as 'emancipatory self-organisation' or to speak in Marx's terms: self-organisation to overthrow every relation in which humankind is being subjugated. You can verbally differentiate yourself better that way. On the other hand, our form of self-organisation was always one that behaved very chaotically, that expressed itself as anti-economical in both the best and worst cases. We often had this debate from fear that we would become role models for Volkswagen managers. Nevertheless, differences to neoliberal self-organisation naturally emerge.

Within capital and labour, in the reform of capitalism, there are simply intersections and there have to be intersections, because there is always something inherent in the course of capitalism that implies great upheaval, repeatedly overthrowing old tactics, strategies, cultures and behavioural patterns. Something very liberating also lies in this moment, a potentiality that has a revolutionary perspective – one only has to take these moments and radicalise them in the direction of the liberation of society. These are all big words, but I believe you cannot really go any smaller – it is about distinguishing oneself pretty precisely and at the same time examining the interrelations, without letting oneself become paralysed by discussions about why the economy has incorporated our beloved self-organisation. It is a process in which you hurl tactics and practice into a reciprocal relation with each other. Capitalism has certainly learned from the strategies of the new social movement, there are definitely tactics and strategies that have gone into the relation of capital, exactly like we've profited from the productivity of this capitalist society. So I don't think that one can so clearly say that this is a 'pure' and 'liberating' self-organisation, and that the other kind is neoliberal capitalist organization, from which we are firstly free, and secondly autonomous and eternally protected. I don't want to say that it is give and take, it is a contradictory relationship.

Strategies

This contradictoriness manifests itself in the strategy of over-affirmation that we applied for My Academy. Over-affirmation could be regarded as a metaphor for the relationship of a political intervention, of a critique of the relationships, and simultaneously of the methods, of assimilating the forms and language of your opponent, of radicalising, leading you into extremes and thereby generating confusion and disquiet, which does not, however, allow itself to be diverted into direct repression.

We would never even have managed to get out of the library unmolested if we had not adopted this language to an absurd degree. This is a moment of self-empowerment that is maybe more important for the inside, for the group or the context than for the measurable relevance that this action had for a debate at the

Academy. That's why we also drove My Academy in various directions, in order to develop various relevancies in various directions. On the one hand, the interventional, performative, over-affirmative side, and on the other, the side where, completely classically, we also distributed information in swathes that we had compiled in the course of our research at the academy.

It was always about broadcasting in as many directions as possible.

Above all, the over-affirmation was also important for bringing the possibility of this form of self-empowerment directly into experience. For proving with this kind of performance that this society is constructed, changeable and re-organisable, that a revolutionary perspective is also possible without any party and state that legitimises and executes it, that another society is possible. Over-affirmation was one method. Within this project, over-affirmation was a method which retrospectively was, of course, the most spectacular element; the element which is now the easiest to communicate over long distances, whereas the educational and organisational work is rather left behind, or takes a back seat from the outside at least.

Self-understanding

We didn't work, as a tight-knit group on one topic, in order to become experts, we wanted to work in various fields, in various formats, with various intensities. We refer to this form of working and organising as eruption. Our structure should make this possible, and its towards this that we directed our organisation.

Translated from German by Rosa Kerosene

Action Against Private Equity Firms
London, July 17th 2008

PECAN Collective

Why target finance capital?

The current political moment is marked by questioning where power is located. It could be argued that transnational regulatory bodies, such as the WTO and IMF, do not have the power they once did; the IMF faces a budget deficit (*International Herald Tribune*, 8/4/2008) and the failure of WTO talks in July have lead some commentators to speculate that it might be losing its influence in regulating global trade (*Der Spiegel*, 30/7/2008). The PECAN collective felt that one possible response would be to target finance capital and to make visible the largely secretive deals that often take place. We were also angered by the government's overall subservience to the ultra-wealthy and the financial sector, and specifically the tax schemes penalising those at the very bottom (as in the elimination of the 10p tax band) while allowing those at the top to get away with literally billions in unpaid taxes.

Who are we?

The Private Equity Creative Action Network is a growing network of labour, environmental and cultural organisers from several different countries, who have been exploring issues of precarity, debt and the emerging crisis of food, fuel and finance. This network has been evolving through organising solidarity actions with labour struggles, while deepening our analysis and critique of capitalism and the need for radical change, in order to win real justice for workers and ensuring the survival of our planet.

What are private equity firms?

Private equity firms use money from pension funds and wealthy investors, and use this to purchase companies with the express purpose of selling them on for a profit. After they have bought the companies, which are then removed from public trading; hence 'private', they can operate free of accountability. They also put them in debt so they no longer pay taxes. They then pay off the debt by 'restructuring' the companies: cutting costs, selling off assets, sacking workers and outsourcing the jobs. In other words, risks are socialised as pension funds are used to pay for deals that could (ironically) potentially threaten the jobs of pension holders. The volume of private equity deals has grown 600% in the last five years. In 2006, private equity firms spent US$725 billion buying out companies. Today, they can potentially mobilise more than US$2 trillion – enough to buy McDonalds 38 times over!

About our action

Ours took place as part of a global day of action against private equity firms, with actions taking place in 25 countries. We began with a march from Trafalgar Square to the KKR's[1] headquarters, to the tune of the Beatles' 'The Taxman' and Pink Floyd's 'Money'. We carried a giant invoice to KKR from the £225 million owed to the UK government in unpaid taxes from their purchase of Boots, the pharmacy chain. There were giant golden number-shaped balloons and props representing schools, houses and trees: the 'public goods and services' that £225 million would have paid for. The 4 metre long invoice was unveiled outside the KKR headquarters (an unobtrusive, but sinister building near Buckingham Palace, which also houses the headquarters of arms dealer BAE Systems). We demanded that KKR's executives come out of the building and receive it. A group of ten KKR representatives in suits stood in the lobby, behind locked doors and police, watching the group. Finally, two KKR representatives came outside and received their invoice from the British public.

---

[1] KKR is one of the oldest and largest private equity firms in the world.

References:

www.privateequitysucks.com

http://www.july17action.org/

"IMF to Sell Gold as It Faces Budget Deficit". *International Herald Tribune*, 8 April 2008.
http://www.iht.com/articles/2008/04/08/business/gold.php

"WTO Failure Reflects Changing Global Power Relations". *Der Spiegel*, 30 July 2008.
http://www.spiegel.de/international/world/0,1518,569027,00.html

Beneath the New Bohemia

Rebecca Gordon Nesbitt

On 1 April 2007, the Cultural and Leisure Services department of Glasgow City Council became Culture and Sport Glasgow (CSG), a private company with charitable status and a separate trading arm. This strongly-contested departure from the New Labour council was spearheaded by Bridget McConnell, wife of the First Minister of Scotland (whose New Labour party would be deposed from control of the Scottish Government exactly one month later). And, although it appeared to pass through all the correct layers of council bureaucracy, being finally approved on 2 February, the company had already been registered and charitable status applied for on 22 December 2006.

The hasty creation of a company to manage culture and leisure in Glasgow – including the city's libraries, museums and galleries (thereby affecting, directly or indirectly, most of the major cultural venues in the city) – prompted research into the overlapping networks and interests of its key personnel. Aside from the six councillors invited to take up places on the board of the main company, this quickly revealed the remaining seats on both boards to be dominated by business interests, including all the major Scottish banks and some of the more nefarious think tanks – Demos, the Social Market Foundation and the Futures Forum.

This mapping of social elites is not a new approach, but what is unusual about CSG is the presence on its board of six elected councillors. While giving the company a veneer of public accountability, their interests proved the most telling when considering its likely future trajectory. Alongside the former Council Business Manager and the City Treasurer (managing the council's £1.3 billion debt which costs £90 million in interest every year) sit the Leader of the Council and the former Lord Provost (the Scottish equivalent of Lord Mayor). Their combined influence points directly to the city's misguided tourism and regeneration strategy, which spectacularly ignores the stifling poverty that grips the city. Like the creative industries agenda on which it is predicated at a local and national level, this model considers culture solely in terms of its use value, with the business people and bureaucrats at the helm having little sympathy towards creative practice beyond the cultural capital it confers upon them. In the process of the city's culture becoming instrumentalised, employees of the new company are being offered worse pay terms than their former council colleagues.

Early indications are that the new company does not prize freedom of expression very highly, which should serve as a warning to the city's creative communities. When this research was published in the summer 2008 issue of Variant,[1] it provoked a vociferous reaction from CSG Media Manager, James Doherty. He immediately threatened the magazine with legal action on the basis of the article's alleged 'inaccuracies and potentially defamatory statements.' A subsequent list showed these objections to be largely trivial and easily rebutted by evidence available in the public domain.[2] Interestingly, none of Doherty's objections related to the main thrust of the argument, about the presumed direction of the city's culture or the intrusion of private interests, but they did lean heavily on his rejection of the use of previous newspaper articles as source material. Around the same time, Variant was banned from all CSG venues and James Doherty was discovered to be President of the National Union of Journalists.

While the creation of Culture and Sport Glasgow reads as a desperate attempt by the New Labour elite to cling onto power, it remains to be seen what impact it will have on cultural provision in the city. Where earlier versions of neoliberalism have repressively tolerated critique, the relatively measured analysis of privatised culture outlined above seemed to prompt a disproportionate reaction. As a safeguard against future negative publicity and a sign of things to come, Culture and Sport Glasgow has now assumed responsibility for research at Glasgow's main newspapers.[3]

Footnotes:

[1] http://www.variant.randomstate.org/pdfs/issue32/Variant32RGN.pdf

[2] http://www.variant.randomstate.org/clarcor.html

[3] See Catherine Watson, 'Bad News for Media Libraries?' *Gazette*, 8-21 August, 2008 (published by the Chartered Institute of Library and Information Professionals). Research is currently being undertaken by Culture and Sport Glasgow, via its Mitchell Library, for the *Herald*, *Sunday Herald* and *Evening Times*, part of SMG Publishing, which was bought by the media conglomerate, Newsquest (http://www.newsquest.co.uk), in 2003. Newsquest runs more than three hundred local newspapers and is, in turn, a subsidiary of the American 'information company' Gannet http://www.gannett.com/ which, amongst other things, publishes *USA Today*.

What It Means to Lose: The Harassment of the Leftist Press in Saint Petersburg

Chto Delat Platform

August 27, 2008 was a dark day for Petersburg's leftist community. Marxist activist Alexei Drozdov was arrested by two policemen while distributing his self-produced leaflet *For Worker Power* to dockers outside the Port of Saint Petersburg. In all likelihood, an argument with a worker about an article in Drozdov's broadsheet – "A 'Coercive' Peace," in which Drozdov takes a critical stance toward Russian actions in South Ossetia and Georgia – led to Drozdov's being reported to the police. His nearly 24-hour whirlwind tour of what passes for a criminal justice system in Russia was typical of what, during the Putin years, has become the standard MO for intimidating activists. A judge eventually sentenced him (to a 500-ruble fine) for "petty hooliganism" – i.e. swearing and ignoring the instructions of the arresting officers. This is the standard charge leveled against public protesters: the Russian Constitution still formally protects free speech. After his hearing, the policemen accompanying Drozdov refused to let him go, however, threatening to re-arrest him if he resisted. Apparently, the police hope to pin a more serious charge – political extremism – on Drozdov and his paper, and they thus wanted more of their higher-ups to have a verbal go at him. (For Drozdov's account of his arrest, see chtodelat.wordpress.com)

Meanwhile, police were searching the Pole Star printing plant, where *For Worker Power* is printed. There they confiscated the newest issue of another leftist publication – *Chto Delat?/What Is To Be Done?*, which is produced by an eponymous group of activists, artists, and philosophers from Petersburg and Moscow. They also found Dmitry Vilensky, the newspaper's editor, who had come to the plant to pick up the new edition ("What Does It Mean to Lose? The Experience of Perestroika") before traveling to Copenhagen, where the paper was to be have been part of a Chto Delat installation at the U-Turn Quadrennial. Vilensky was questioned the next day by police investigators, who were particularly intrigued by the words of the chorus in the screenplay to *Perestroika-Songspiel*, a Brechtian video-opera set after the defeat of the August 1991 coup. The chorus foresees that the naïveté of liberals, the greed of businessmen, and the ferocity of the mafia and a resurgent KGB (FSB) would quickly combine to nullify Russia's experiment in grass roots democratic renewal. (You can read the entire newspaper at www.chtodelat.org.) This, apparently, was enough for a local district attorney to order an inquest into whether *Chto Delat* (along with *For Worker Power*) had violated the law against "extremism," which has been indiscriminately applied in recent years to malcontents ranging from the now-banned National Bolshevik Party to peace activists, liberal oppositionists, Russian Islamists, neo-Nazis and provincial bloggers.

Whatever the outcome of the prosecutor's inquest, it is clear that the current regime – which combines some of the worst features of neoliberalism and Russian authoritarianism – is jealous to guard its near-monopoly on political action and discourse, even against the not-so-numerous voices of Russia's embattled left. After all, it has everything to lose.

"REFFEN" – a living state of optimism

Joen P-Vedel

It all started on Saturday, the 31st of May, when more than eight hundred people walked from the inner city of Copenhagen to Christianshavn, under the slogan "THEY TEAR DOWN, WE BUILD UP!" After the eviction and demolition of Ungdomshuset (the Youth House) in March 2007 and the growing pressure for a 'normalization' of Christiania (our right-wing government is seeking to close it down and transform it into a paradise for the property-owning class), this looked like yet another demonstration for "Flere Fristeder" ("more free spaces"), but something was different.

As the demo reached Refshalevej, which runs along the water behind Christiania, we found big piles of materials and tools distributed at the side of the street, free for everyone to use. Euphoric in the summer heat, people began building; houses grew up between the reed and on platforms in the water, a stage and a kitchen, an info board, a bar and several roadblocks, bridges and tripods. At the same time, people in tents and caravans came to set up camp in order to be part of it all. Quickly, it began to look the way we wanted it to; a NEW 'free space' full of people of all ages and from so many different backgrounds. This was NOT a part of Christiania, not a new Ungdomshus, not a guerilla-garden, but a fresh element in our struggle to keep and expand these places, this was something new and more or less unplanned, a project or an action carried out in the 'here and now'. Instead of dreaming of, and planning for the future, we were building in the present. Instead of always defending our 'old free spaces', a much more diverse group of people/activists came together to go on the offensive at a time of great pressure. The means were a flat structure with direct democracy and common assemblies as the ruling power. There was no hierarchy and no closed groups, but mutual respect, shared interests, great weather (important!) and support and love from our neighbour and biggest inspiration, Christiania.

The time and place for the whole thing was perfect. Christiania was deeply involved in negotiations with the state regarding their future – and possible riots just outside its gates were not what the police were looking for. Furthermore, we were in a grey zone between three different authorities: the state, the harbor and the city council. None approved of what we were doing nor could they figure out who should act on the squat. For once, it seemed that we were benefiting from the bureaucracy, since nothing could be done before the three administrations had reached an agreement. In the meantime, we continued to build and bring in huge amounts of material from dumps and building sites all over Copenhagen.

The number of houses and constructions in the street and on rafts in the water was increasing, as was the number of people that took up residency. Every night there was free food, a film screening, a band performing, a circus show or a quiet guitar by the fire. The diversity of people had never been so great for a squat action, and it took some time to find out how and when we should meet and talk. This was also evident in the many different names the street had, depending on who was talking: "Reffen", "Vejen" (the street), "Haveje", "Frikommunen" (the free commune), "Kommunitetet Refshalevej" (the community of Refshalevej), "D. I. Refshale. Y". We never did find a common name. In the press, we were mostly known as the "Constructors". The focus for all was to build and the more stuff we could get onto rafts the better, the underlying idea being that we could always move on using the Copenhagen waterways. Many people came to see what we were up to, including the press, architects, city planners and authorities. The police also showed up once in a while with cameras to document what was going on, a few times by helicopter. They saw that a new kind of 'building boom' had started and it was moving fast.

Each day on Refshalevej was a victory to us – no one ever thought that we would be able to take it as far as we did. Sometimes while hammering and dreaming, one could even get the feeling that the City of Copenhagen approved of what we were doing, that the Municipality saw the potential in our process-based approach, that they suddenly understood that not all architecture and public space has to be designed for specific segments of the population with specific behavior and a specific profit-oriented wallet. BUT then one morning we woke up to the first notice that an eviction would take place if we didn't clear out. At first this was ignored, while the community continued to expand. A second notice came nine days later and a large number of people left that time. Some then expected the police to turn up in riot gear and we could only emphasize to the public, and some worried residents from Christiania, that we were engaged in 'a non-violent living-experiment' and that we would not defend it by force or aggression. And so it happened: On the morning of the 15th of July, the police blocked both ends of Refshalevej and workers from the municipality demolished the houses and rafts with big cranes. At the time they went in, there were only a few residents in the houses; most of them left voluntarily.

This was the end of a temporary anarchist zone, a one and a half month long living state of optimism for a future in which we can all participate, a showcase to politicians, architects and city planners of the different ways one can choose to live, a direct intervention in the world at a time where most things we say and do are silenced or ignored. The ideological basis may not have been rock-solid or agreed on by all, this was something to be developed, but we gave it our best through participation, improvisation, collaboration and most importantly: a great joy in the moment of creating.

Precarious Labor: A Feminist Viewpoint

Silvia Federici

Precarious work is a central concept in movement discussions of the capitalist reorganization of work and class relations in today's global economy. Silvia Federici analyzes the potential and limits of this concept as an analytical and organizational tool. She claims reproductive labor is a hidden continent of work and struggle the movement must recognize in its political work, if it is to address the key questions we face in organizing for an alternative to capitalist society. How do we struggle over reproductive labor without destroying ourselves and our communities? How do we create a self-reproducing movement? How do we overcome the sexual, racial and generational hierarchies built upon the wage?

This lecture took place on 28 October 2006 at Bluestockings Radical Bookstore in New York City, 172 Allen Street as part of the "This is Forever: From Inquiry to Refusal Discussion Series".

Tonight, I will present a critique of the theory of precarious labor that has been developed by Italian Autonomist Marxists, with particular reference to the work of Antonio Negri, Paolo Virno, and also Michael Hardt. I call it a theory, because the views that Negri and others have articulated go beyond the description of changes in the organization of work that have taken place in the 1980s and 1990s in conjunction with the globalization process – such as the 'precarization of work', the fact that work relations are becoming more discontinuous, the introduction of 'flexy time,' and the increasing fragmentation of the work experience. Their view on precarious labor presents a whole perspective on what capitalism is and what the nature of the struggle today is. It is important to add that these are not simply the ideas of a few intellectuals, but theories that have circulated widely within the Italian movement for a number of years, and have recently also become more influential in the United States, and in this sense they have become more relevant to us.

The history and origin of precarious labor and immaterial labor theory

My first premise is that the question of precarious labor must definitely be on our agenda. Not only has our relationship to waged work become more discontinuous, but a discussion of precarious labor is crucial for our understanding of how we can go beyond capitalism. The theories that I discuss capture important aspects of the developments that have taken place in the organization of work; but they also bring us back to a male-centric conception of work and social struggle. I will now discuss those elements in this theory that are most relevant to my critique.

An important premise in the Italian Autonomists' theory of precarious labor is that the precarization of work, from the late 1970s to present, has been a capitalist response to the class struggle of the 1960s, a struggle that was centered on the refusal of work, as expressed in the slogan 'more money less work'. It was a response to a cycle of struggle that challenged the capitalist command over labor, in a sense realizing the workers' refusal of the capitalist work discipline, the refusal of a life organized by the needs of capitalist production, a life spent in a factory or in the office.

Another important theme is that the precarization of work relations is deeply rooted in another shift that has taken place with the restructuring of production in the 1980s. This is the shift from industrial labor to what Negri and Virno call 'immaterial labor'. Negri and others have argued that the restructuring of production that has taken place in the 1980s and 1990s in response to the struggles of the 1960s has begun a process whereby industrial labor is to be replaced by a different type of work, in the same way as industrial labor replaced agricultural work. They call the new type of work 'immaterial labor', because they claim that with the computer and information revolutions, the dominant form of work has changed. As a tendency, the dominant form of work in today's capitalism is work that does not produce physical objects, but information, ideas, states of being, relations.

In other words, industrial work – which was hegemonic in the previous phase of capitalist development – is now becoming less important; it is no longer the engine of capitalist development. In its place, we find 'immaterial labor', which is essentially cultural work, cognitive work, info work.

Italian Autonomists believe that the precarization of work and the appearance of immaterial labor fulfill the prediction Marx made in the *Grundrisse*, in a famous section on machines. In this section, Marx states that with the development of capitalism, less and less capitalist production relies on living labor and more and more on the integration of science, knowledge and technology in the production process as the engines of accumulation. Virno and Negri see the shift to precarious labor as fulfilling this prediction, about capitalism's historic trend. Thus, the importance of cognitive work and the development of computer work in our time lies in the fact that they are seen as part of a historic trend of capitalism towards the reduction of work.

The precarity of labor is rooted in the new forms of production. Presumably, the shift to immaterial labor generates a precarization of work relations, because the structure of cognitive work is different from that of industrial, physical work. Cognitive and info work rely less on the continuous physical presence of the worker in what was the traditional workplace. The rhythms of work are much more intermittent, fluid and discontinuous.

In sum, the development of precarious labor and shift to immaterial labor are not, for Negri and other Autonomist Marxists, a completely negative phenomenon. On the contrary, they are seen as expressions of a trend towards the reduction of work, and therefore the reduction of exploitation, resulting from capitalist development in response to the class struggle.

This means that the development of the productive forces today is already giving us a glimpse of a world in which work can be transcended; in which we will liberate ourselves from the necessity to work and enter a new realm of freedom.

Autonomous Marxists believe this development is also creating a new kind of "common", originating from the fact that immaterial labor presumably represents a leap in the socialization and homogenization of work. The idea is that differences between types of work that once were all important (e.g. productive/reproductive work; agricultural/industrial/'affective labor') are erased, as all types of work (as a tendency) become assimilated, for all begin to incorporate cognitive work. Moreover, all activities are increasingly subsumed under capitalist development, they all serve to the accumulation process, as society becomes an immense factory. Thus, e.g. the distinction between productive and unproductive labor also vanishes.

This means that capitalism is not only leading us beyond labor, but it is creating the conditions for the "commonization" of our work experience, where the divisions are beginning to crumble.

We can see why these theories have become popular. They have utopian elements especially attractive to cognitive workers – the 'cognitariat' as Negri and some Italian activists call them. With the new theory, in fact, a new vocabulary has been invented. Instead of the proletariat, we have the 'cognitariat'. Instead of working class, we have the 'Multitude', presumably because the concept of Multitude reveals the unity that is created by the new socialization of work; it expresses the communalization of the work process, the idea that within the work process workers are becoming more homogenized. For all forms of work incorporate elements of cognitive work, of computer work, communication work and so forth.

As I said, this theory has gained much popularity, because there is a generation of young activists, with years of schooling and degrees who are now employed in precarious ways in different parts of the culture industry or the knowledge-production industry. Among them, these theories are very popular, because they tell them that despite the misery and exploitation we are experiencing, we are nevertheless moving towards a higher level of production and social relations. This is a generation of workers who look at the "nine to five" routine as a prison sentence. They see their precariousness as giving them new possibilities. And they have possibilities their parents did not have or dreamed of. The male youth of today (e.g.) is not as disciplined as their parents who could expect that their wife or partners would depend of them economically. Now they can count on social relationships involving much less financial dependence. Most women have autonomous access to the wage and often refuse to have children.

So this theory is appealing for the new generation of activists who, despite the difficulties resulting from precarious labor, see within it certain possibilities. They want to start from there. They are not interested in a struggle for full employment. But there is also a difference here between Europe and the US. In Italy e.g. there is among the movement, a demand for a guaranteed income. They call it 'flex security'. They say, 'we are without a job, we are precarious, because capitalism needs us to be, so they should pay for it'. There have been various days of mobilization, especially on May 1st, centered on this demand for a guaranteed income. In Milan, on May Day this year, movement people paraded 'San Precario', the patron saint of the precarious worker. The ironic icon is featured in rallies and demonstrations centered on this question of precarity.

Critique of precarious labor

I will now shift to my critique of these theories – a critique from a feminist viewpoint. In developing my critique, I don't want to minimize the importance of the theories I am discussing. They have been inspired by much political organizing and striving to make sense of the changes that have taken place in the organization of work, which has affected all our lives. In Italy, in recent years, precarious labor has been one of the main terrains of mobilization together with the struggle for immigrant rights.

I do not want to minimize the work that is taking place around issues of precarity. Clearly, what we have seen in the last decade is a new kind of struggle. A new kind of organizing is taking place, breaking away from the confines of the traditional workplace. Where the workplace was the factory or the office, we now see a kind of struggle that goes out of the factory to the 'territory', connecting different places of work and building movements and organizations rooted in the territory. The theories of precarious labor are trying to account for the aspects of novelty in the organization of work and struggle; trying to understand the emergent forms of organization.

This is very important. At the same time, I think that what I called precarious labor theory has serious flaws that I already hinted at in my presentation. I will outline them and then discuss the question of alternatives.

My first criticism is that this theory is built on a faulty understanding of how capitalism works. It sees capitalist development as moving towards higher forms of production and labor. In *Multitude*, Negri and Hardt actually write that labor is becoming more 'intelligent'. The assumption is that the capitalist organization of work and capitalist development are already creating the conditions for the overcoming of exploitation. Presumably, at one point capitalism, the shell that keeps society going, will break up and the potentialities that have grown within it will be liberated. There is an assumption that that process is already at work in the present organization of production. In my view, this is a misunderstanding of the effects of the restructuring produced by capitalist globalization and the neo-liberal turn.

What Negri and Hardt do not see is that the tremendous leap in technology, required by the computerization of work and the integration of information into the work process, *has been paid at the cost of a tremendous increase in exploitation at the other end of the process.* There is a continuum between the computer worker and the worker in the Congo who digs coltan with his hands trying to seek out a living after being expropriated, pauperized, by repeated rounds of structural adjustment and repeated theft of his community's land and natural sources.

The fundamental principle is that capitalist development is always, at the same time, a process of underdevelopment. Maria Mies describes it eloquently in her work: "What appears as development in one part of the capitalist faction is underdevelopment in another part."

This connection is completely ignored in this theory; in fact and the whole theory is permeated by the illusion that the work process is bringing us together. When Negri and Hardt speak of the 'becoming common' of work and use the concept of the Multitude to indicate the new commonism that is built through the development of the productive forces, I believe they are blind to much of what is happening with the world's proletariat.

They are blind to not see the capitalist destruction of lives and the ecological environment. They don't see that the restructuring of production has aimed at restructuring and deepening the divisions within the working class, rather than erasing them. The idea that the development of the microchip is creating new commons is misleading. Communalism can only be a product of struggle, not of capitalist production.

One of my criticisms of Negri and Hardt is that they seem to believe that the capitalist organization of work is the expression of a higher rationality and that capitalist development is necessary to create the material conditions for communism. This belief is at the center of precarious labor theory. We could discuss here whether it represents Marx's thinking or not. Certainly the *Communist Manifesto* speaks of capitalism in these terms and the same is true of some sections of the *Grundrisse*. But it is not clear this was a dominant theme in Marx's work, not in *Capital* at least.

Precarious labor and reproductive work

Another criticism I have against the precarious labor theory is that it presents itself as gender neutral. It assumes that the reorganization of production is doing away with the power relations and hierarchies that exist within the working class on the basis of race, gender and age, and therefore, it is not concerned with addressing these power relations; it does not have the theoretical and political tools to think about how to tackle them. There is no discussion in Negri, Virno and Hardt of how the wage has been and continues to be used to organize these divisions, and how, therefore, we must approach the wage struggle so that it does not become an instrument of further divisions, but instead can help us undermine them. To me, this is one of the main issues we must address in the movement.

The concept of the "Multitude" suggests that all divisions within the working class are gone or are no longer politically relevant. But this is obviously an illusion. Some feminists have pointed out that precarious labor is not a new phenomenon. Women always had a precarious relation to waged labor. But this critique goes far enough.

My concern is that the Negrian theory of precarious labor ignores, bypasses, one of the most important contributions of feminist theory and struggle, which is the redefinition of work, and the recognition of women's unpaid reproductive labor as a key source of capitalist accumulation. In redefining housework as WORK, as not a personal service, but the work that produces and reproduces labor power, feminists have uncovered a new crucial ground of exploitation that Marx and Marxist theory completely ignored. All of the important political insights contained in those analyses are now brushed aside as if they were of no relevance to an understanding of the present organization of production.

There is a faint echo of the feminist analysis – a lip service paid to it – in the inclusion of so-called "affective labor" in the range of work activities qualifying as 'immaterial labor'. However, the best Negri and Hardt can come up with is the case of women who work as flight attendants or in the food service industry, whom they call 'affective laborers', because they are expected to smile at their customers.

But what is 'affective labor'? And why is it included in the theory of immaterial labor? I imagine it is included, because – presumably – it does not produce tangible products but 'states of being', that is, it produces feelings. Again, to put it crudely, I think this is a bone thrown to feminism, which now is a perspective that has some social backing and can no longer be ignored.

But the concept of "affective labor" strips the feminist analysis of housework of all its demystifying power. In fact, it brings reproductive work back into the world of mystification, suggesting that reproducing people is just a matter of producing 'emotions', 'feelings'. It used to be called a 'labor of love'; Negri and Hardt instead have discovered 'affection'.

The feminist analysis of the function of the sexual division of labor, the function of gender hierarchies, the analysis of the way capitalism has used the wage to mobilize women's work in the reproduction of the labor force – all of this is lost under the label of 'affective labor'.

That this feminist analysis is ignored in the work of Negri and Hardt confirms my suspicions that this theory expresses the interests of a select group of workers, even though it presumes to speak to all workers, all merged in the great caldron of the Multitude. In reality, the theory of precarious and immaterial labor speaks to the situation and interests of workers, working at the highest level of capitalistic technology. Its disinterest in reproductive labor, and its presumption that all labor forms a common, hides the fact that it is concerned with the most privileged section of the working class. This means it is not a theory we can use to build a truly self-reproducing movement.

For this task, the lesson of the feminist movement is still crucial today. Feminists in the 1970s tried to understand the roots of women's oppression, of women's exploitation and gender hierarchies. They describe them as stemming from a unequal division of labor, forcing women to work for the reproduction of the working class. This analysis was basis of a radical social critique, the implications of which still have to be understood and developed to their full potential.

When we said that housework is actually work for capital, that although it is unpaid work, it contributes to the accumulation of capital, we established something extremely important about the nature of capitalism as a system of production. *We established that capitalism is built on an immense amount of unpaid labor, that it is not built exclusively or primarily on contractual relations; that the wage relation hides the unpaid, slave-like nature of so much of the work upon which capital accumulation is premised.*

Also, when we said that housework is the work that reproduces not just 'life', but 'labor-power', we began to separate two different spheres of our lives and work that seemed inextricably connected. We became able to conceive of a fight against housework, now understood as the reproduction of labor-power, the reproduction of the most important commodity capital has: the worker's 'capacity to work', the worker's capacity to be exploited. In other words, by recognizing that what we call 'reproductive labor' is a terrain of accumulation, and therefore, a terrain of exploitation, we were able to also see reproduction as a terrain of struggle, and very importantly, *conceive of an anti-capitalist struggle against reproductive labor that would not destroy ourselves or our communities.*

How do you struggle over/against reproductive work? It is not the same as struggling in the traditional factory setting, against for instance, the speed of an assembly line, because at the other end of your struggle there are people, not things. Once we say that reproductive work is a terrain of struggle, we have to first immediately confront the question of how we struggle on this terrain without destroying the people you care for. This is a problem mothers, as well as teachers and nurses, know very well.

This is why it is crucial to be able to make a separation between the creation of human beings and our reproduction of them as labor-power, as future workers, who therefore have to be trained, not necessarily according to their needs and desires, to be disciplined and regimented in a particular fashion.

It was important for feminists to see, for example, that much housework and child-rearing is work of policing our children, so that they will conform to a particular work discipline. We, thus, began to see that by refusing broad areas of work, we not only could liberate ourselves, but could also liberate our children. We saw that our struggle was not at the expense of the people we cared for, though we may skip preparing some meals or cleaning the floor. Actually our refusal opened the way for their refusal and the process of their liberation.

Once we saw that rather than reproducing life we were expanding capitalist accumulation and began to define reproductive labor as work for capital, we also opened the possibility of a process of recomposition among women.

Think, for example, of the prostitute movement, which we now call the 'sex workers' movement. In Europe, the origins of this movement must be traced back to 1975 when a number of sex workers in Paris occupied a church, in protest against a new zoning regulation, which they saw as an attack on their safety. There was a clear connection between that struggle, which soon spread throughout Europe and the United States, and the feminist movement's rethinking and challenging of housework. The ability to say that sexuality for women has been work has lead to a whole new way of thinking about sexual relationships, including gay relations. Because of the feminist movement and the gay movement, we have begun to think about the ways in which capitalism has exploited our sexuality, and made it 'productive'.

In conclusion, it was a major breakthrough that women would begin to understand unpaid labor and the production that goes on in the home, as well as outside of the home, as the reproduction of the work force. This has allowed a rethinking of every aspect of everyday life – child-raising, relationships between men and women, homosexual relationships, sexuality in general – in relation to capitalist exploitation and accumulation.

Creating self-reproducing movements

As every aspect of everyday life was re-understood in its potential for liberation and exploitation, we saw the many ways in which women and women's struggles are connected. We realized the possibility of 'alliances' we had not imagined, and by the same token, the possibility of bridging the divisions that have been created among women, also on the basis of age, race, sexual preference.

We cannot build a movement that is sustainable without an understanding of these power relations. We also need to learn from the feminist analysis of reproductive work, because no movement can survive unless it is concerned with the reproduction of its members. This is one of the weaknesses of the social justice movement in the US.
We go to demonstrations, we build events, and this becomes the peak of

our struggle. The analysis of how we reproduce these movements, how we reproduce ourselves is not at the center of movement-organizing. It has to be. We need to go to back to the historical tradition of working class organizing 'mutual aid', and rethink that experience, not necessarily because we want to reproduce it, but to draw inspiration from it for the present.

We need to build a movement that puts on its agenda its own reproduction. The anti-capitalist struggle has to create forms of support and has to have the ability to collectively build forms of reproduction.

We have to ensure that we do not only confront capital at the time of the demonstration, but that we confront it collectively at every moment of our lives. What is happening internationally proves that only when you have these forms of collective reproduction, when you have communities that reproduce themselves collectively, you have struggles that are moving in a very radical way against the established order, as for example, the struggle of indigenous people in Bolivia against water privatization or in Ecuador against the oil companies' destruction of indigenous land.

I want to close by saying, if we look at the example of the struggles in Oaxaca, Bolivia, and Ecuador, we see that the most radical confrontations are not created by the intellectual or cognitive workers or by virtue of the Internet's common. What gave strength to the people of Oaxaca was the profound solidarity that tied them to each other – a solidarity for instance that made indigenous people from every part of the state to come to the support of the 'maestros', whom they saw as members of their communities. In Bolivia, too, the people who reversed the privatization of water had a long tradition of communal struggle. Building this solidarity, understanding how we can overcome the divisions between us, is a task that must be placed on the agenda. In conclusion, then, the main problem of precarious labor theory is that it does not give us the tools to overcome the way we are being divided. But these divisions, which are continuously recreated, are our fundamental weakness with regard to our capacity to resist exploitation and create an equitable society.

Previously published in: *In The Middle Of A Whirlwind*, coordinated by TEAM COLORS [militant research collective]. Published by: *The Journal of Aesthetics & Protest Press*. 2008. www.inthe middleofawhirlwind.info

The Sadness of Post-Workerism
or "Art and Immaterial Labour" Conference:
a Sort of Review
(Tate Britain, Saturday 19 January, 2008)

by David Graeber

On the 19th of January, several of the heavyweights of Italian post-Workerist theory – Toni Negri, Bifo Berardi, Maurizio Lazzarato and Judith Revel – appeared at the Tate Britain to talk about art. This is a review.

Or, it is a review in a certain sense. I want to give an account of what happened. But I also want to talk about why I think what happened was interesting and important. For me, at least, this means addressing not only what was said, but just as much perhaps, what wasn't; and asking questions like "why immaterial labor?", and "why did it make sense to all concerned, to bring a group of revolutionary theorists over from Italy to talk about art history in the first place?" Asking these questions will allow me to make some much broader points about the nature of art, politics, history and social theory, which I like to think are at least as interesting and potentially revealing as what happened in the actual debate.

What happened

Here's a very brief summary:
The session was organized by Peter Osborne, along with a number of other scholars at Middlesex College involved in the journal *Radical Philosophy*, and Eric Alliez, editor of *Multitudes*. None of the organizers could really be considered part of the art world. Nor were any of the speakers known primarily for what they had to say about things artistic. Everyone seems to have felt they were there to explore slightly new territory. This included, I think, much of the audience. The place was packed, but especially, it seemed, with students and scholars involved in some way with post-graduate education – especially where it interfaced with the culture industry. Among many scholars, of course, there were very big names, celebrities, even something close to rock stars. Many of the graduate students in particular were no doubt there in part just for the opportunity to finally see figures, whose ideas they'd been debating for most of their intellectual careers, revealed to them in the flesh: to see what they looked like, what kind of clothes they wore, how they held themselves and spoke and moved. Perhaps even to mill about in the pub afterwards and rub shoulders.

This is always part of the pleasure of the event. Certainly this was part of the pleasure for me. Great theorists are almost always, in a certain sense, performers. Even if you've seen photographs, it never conveys a full sense of who they are; and when you do get a sense of who they are, returning to read their work with one's new, personal sense of the author tends to be an entirely different experience. It was interesting to observe Lazzarato's smooth head and excellent moustache; Revel's poise and energy; Bifo's hair – sort of Warhol meets Jacques Derrida – not to mention the way he seemed to walk as if floating a half inch above the pavement; Negri's almost sheepishness at his inability to pronounce long English words, which made him seem shy and almost boyish. I had never really had a sense of what any of these people were like and I walked away, oddly, with much more respect for them as people. This is partly, no doubt, because anyone who you know largely through obscurely written texts that some treat with an almost mystical adulation tends to become, in one's imagination, rather an arrogant person, self-important, someone who thinks oneself a kind of minor rock star, perhaps, since they are treated as such – even if within a very narrow circle. Events like this remind one just how narrow the circle of such celebrity can often be. These were people who certainly were comfortable in the spotlight. But otherwise, their conditions of existence obviously in no way resembled that of rock stars. In fact, they were rather modest. Most had paid a significant price for their radical commitments and some continued to do so: Negri is now out of jail of course and settled in a fairly comfortable life on academic and government pensions, but Bifo is a high school teacher (if at a very classy high school) and Lazzarato appears under the dreaded rubric of 'independent scholar'. It's a little shocking to discover scholars of such recognized importance in the domain of ideas could really have received such little institutional recognition, but of course, there is very little connection between the two – especially, when politics is involved.

(Neither were they likely to be walking home with vast troves of money from taking part in this particular event: 500 tickets at £20 each might seem like a bit of money, but once you figure in the cost of the venue, hotels and transportation, the remainder, split four ways, would make for a decidedly modest lecture fee.)

All in all, they seemed to exude an almost wistful feeling of modest, likable people scratching their heads over the knowledge that, twenty years before, struggling side to side with insurrectionary squatters and running pirate radio stations, they would never have imagined ending up quite where they were now, filling the lecture hall of a stodgy British museum with philosophy students eager to hear their opinions about art. The wistfulness was only intensified by the general tenor of the afternoon's discussion, which started off guardedly hopeful about social possibilities in the first half, and then, in the second half, collapsed.

Here's a brief summary of what happened:
MAURIZIO LAZZARATO presented a paper called *"Art, Work and Politics in Disciplinary Societies and Societies of Security"*, in which he talked about Duchamp and Kafka's story Josephine the singing mouse, and explained how the relation of 'art, work and politics' had changed as we pass from Foucault's 'disciplinary society' to his 'society of security'. Duchamp's ready-mades provides a kind of model of a new form of action that lies suspended between what we consider production and management; it is an anti-dialectical model in effect of forms of immaterial labor to follow, which entail just the sort of blurring of boundaries of work and play, art and life that the avant garde had called for, that is opened up in the spaces of freedom that 'societies of security' must necessarily allow, and that any revolutionary challenge to capitalism must embrace.

JUDITH REVEL presented a paper called *"The Material of the Immaterial: Against the Return of Idealisms and New Vitalisms"*, explained that even many of those willing to agree that we are now under a regime of real subsumption to capital do not seem to fully understand the implications: that there is *nothing* outside. This includes those who posit some sort of autonomous life-force, such as Agamben's 'bare life'. Such ideas need to be jettisoned, as also Deleuze's insistence we see desire as a vital energy prior to the constraints of power. Rather, the current moment can be understood only through Foucault, particularly his notion of ethical self-fashioning; this also allows us to see that art is not a series of objects, but a form of critical practice designed to produce ruptures in existing regimes of power

> *A lively discussion* ensued in which everyone seemed happy to declare Agamben defunct, but the Deleuzians fought back bitterly. No clear victor emerged.

BIFO presented a paper called *"Connection/Conjunction"*. He began by talking about Marinetti and Futurism. The twentieth century was the 'century of the future'. But that's over. In the current moment, which is no longer one of conjunction, but of connection, there is no longer a future. Cyber-space is infinite, but cyber-time is most definitively not. The precarity of labor means life is pathologized; and where once Lenin could teeter back and forth from depressive breakdowns to decisive historical action, no such action is now possible, suicide is the only form of effective political action; art and life have fused and it's a disaster; any new wave of radical subjectification is inconceivable now. If there was hope, it is only for some great catastrophe, after which possibly, maybe, everything might change.

> *A confused and depressing discussion* ensued, in which Bifo defended his despair, in a cheerful and charming manner,

admitting that he has abandoned Deleuze for Baudrillard. There's no hope, he says: "I hope that I am wrong."

TONI NEGRI presented a paper called *"Concerning Periodisation in Art: Some Approaches to Art and Immaterial Labour"* which began, as the title implies, with a brief history of how, since the 1840s, artistic trends mirrored changes in the composition of labor. (That part was really quite lucid. Then the words began) Then after '68, we had post-modernism, but now we're beyond that too, all the posts are post now, we're in yet a new phase, Contemporaneity, in which we see the ultimate end of cognitive labor is prosthesis, the simultaneous genesis of person and machine; as biopolitical power it becomes a constant explosion, a vital excess beyond measure, through which the Multitude's powers can take ethical form in the creation of a new global commons. Despite the occasionally explosive metaphors, though, the talk was received as a gesture of quiet, but determined revolutionary optimism opposing itself to Bifo's grandiose gesture of despair – if one diluted, somewhat, by the fact that almost no one in the audience seemed able to completely understand it. While the first, analytical part of the paper was admirably concrete, as soon as it began to talk about revolutionary prospects, it also shifted to a level of abstraction so arcane that it was almost impossible for this listener at least (and I took copious notes!) to figure out what, exactly, any of this would mean in practice.

> *A final discussion was proposed* in which each speaker was asked to sum up. There is a certain reluctance. Lazzarato demurs, he does not want to say anything. "Bifo has made me depressed." Bifo too passes. Negri admits that Bifo has indeed defined the 'heaviest, most burdensome' question of our day, but all is not necessarily lost, rather, a new language is required to even begin to think about such matters. Only Judith Revel picks up the slack and all is not necessarily lost, despite the miserable realities, the power of our indignation is real – the only question is, how to transform that into the Common.

Revel's intervention, however, had something of the air of a desperate attempt to save the day. Everyone left somewhat confused, and a little unsettled. Bifo's collapse of faith was particularly unsettling, because generally he is the very avatar of hope; in fact, even here his manner and argument seemed at almost complete cross-purposes; his every gesture seemed to exude a kind of playful energy, a delight in the fact of existence, that his every word seemed determined to puncture and negate. It was very difficult to know what to make of it.

Instead of trying to take on the arguments point by point – as I said, this is only a sort of review – let me instead throw out some initial thoughts on what the presentations had in common. In other words, I am less interested in entering into the ring and batting around arguments for whether Foucault or Deleuze are better suited for helping us realize the radical potential in the current historical moment, as to ask why such questions are being batted about by Italian revolutionaries, in an art museum, in the first place. Here I can make four initial observations, all of which, at the time, I found mildly surprising:

1) There was almost no discussion of contemporary art. Just about every piece of art discussed was within what might be called the classic avant garde tradition (Dada, Futurism, Duchamp, Abstract Expressionism...) Negri did take his history of art forms up through the 1960s, and Bifo mentioned Banksy. But that was about it.

2) While all of the speakers could be considered Italian Autonomists and they were ostensibly there to discuss immaterial labor, a concept that emerged from the Italian Autonomist tradition, surprisingly few concepts specific to that tradition were deployed. Rather, the theoretical language drew almost exclusively on the familiar heroes of French '68 thought: Michel Foucault, Jean Baudrillard, Deleuze and Guattari... At one point, the editor of *Multitude*, Eric Alliez, in introducing Negri made a point of saying that one of the great achievements of his work was to give a second life to such thinkers, a kind of renewed street cred, by making them seem once again relevant to revolutionary thought.

3) In each case, the presenters used those French thinkers as a tool to create a theory about historical stages – or some cases, imitated them by coming up with an analogous theory of stages of their own. For each, the key question was: what is the right term with which to characterize the present? What makes our time unique? Is it that we have passed from a society of discipline, to one of security or control? Or is it that regimes of conjunction have been replaced by regimes of connection? Have we experienced a passage from formal to real subsumption? Or from modernity to post-modernity? Or have we passed post-modernity, too now, and entered an entirely new phase?

4) All of them were remarkably polite. Dramatically lacking was anything that might provoke discomfort in even the stodgiest Tate Britain curator, or even, really, any of their wealthiest patrons. This is worthy of note, no one can seriously deny the speakers' radical credentials. Most had proved themselves willing to take genuine personal risks at moments when there was any reason to believe some realistic prospect of revolution was afoot. There was

no doubt that, had some portion of London's proletariat risen up in arms during their stay, most if not all, would have immediately reported to the barricades. But since they had not, their attacks or even criticisms were limited to other intellectuals: Badiou, Ranciere, Agamben.

These observations may seem scattershot, but I think taken together they are revealing. Why, for example, would one wish to argue that in the year 2008 we live in a unique historical moment, unlike anything that came before, and then act as if this moment can only really be described through concepts French thinkers developed in the 1960s and 1970s – then illustrate one's points almost exclusively with art created between 1916 and 1922?

This does seem strangely arbitrary but I suspect there is a reason. We might ask: what does the moment of Futurism, Dada, Constructivism and the rest, and French '68 thought, have in common? Actually quite a lot. Each corresponded to a moment of revolution: to adopt Immanuel Wallerstein's terminology, the world revolution of 1917 in one case, and the world revolution of 1968 in the other. Each witnessed an explosion of creativity in which a longstanding European artistic or intellectual Grand Tradition effectively reached the limits of its radical possibilities. That is to say, they marked the last moment at which it was possible to plausibly claim that breaking all the rules – whether violating artistic conventions, or shattering philosophical assumptions – was itself, necessarily, a subversive political act as well.

This is particularly easy to see in the case of the European avant garde. From Duchamp's first readymade in 1914, Hugo Ball's Dada Manifesto and tone poems in 1916, to Malevich's White on White in 1918, culminating in the whole phenomenon of Berlin Dada from 1918 to 1922, one could see revolutionary artists perform, in rapid succession, just about every subversive gesture it was possible to make: from white canvases to automatic writing, theatrical performances designed to incite riots, sacrilegious photo montage, gallery shows in which the public was handed hammers and invited to destroy any piece they took a disfancy to, objects plucked off the street and sacralized as art. All that remained for the Surrealists was to connect a few remaining dots, and the heroic moment was over. One could still do political art, of course, and one could still defy convention. But it became effectively impossible to claim that by doing one you were necessarily doing the other, and increasingly difficult to even try to do both at the same time. It was possible, certainly, to continue in the avant garde tradition without claiming one's work had political implications (as did anyone from Jackson Pollock to Andy Warhol), it was possible to do straight-out political art (like, say, Diego Rivera); one could even (like the Situationists) continue as a revolutionary in the avant garde tradition, but stop making art, but that pretty much exhausted the remaining possibilities.

What happened to continental philosophy after May '68 is quite similar. Assumptions were shattered, grand declarations abounded (the intellectual equivalent of Dada manifestos): the death of Man, of Truth, The Social, reason, dialectics, even Death itself. But the end result was roughly the same. Within a decade, the possible radical positions one could take within the Grand Tradition of post-Cartesian philosophy had been, essentially, exhausted. The heroic moment was over. What's more, it became increasingly difficult to maintain the premise that heroic acts of epistemological subversion were revolutionary or even particularly subversive in any other sense. In fact their effects seemed if anything depoliticizing. Just as purely formal avant garde experiment proved perfectly well suited to grace the homes of conservative bankers, and Surrealist montage to become the language of the advertising industry, so did post-structural theory quickly prove the perfect philosophy for self-satisfied liberal academics with no political engagement at all.

If nothing else this would explain the obsessive-compulsive quality of the constant return to such heroic moments. It is, ultimately, a subtle form of conservatism – or, perhaps one should say conservative radicalism, if such were possible – a nostalgia for the days when it was possible to put on a tin foil suit, shout nonsense verse, and watch staid bourgeois audiences turn into outraged lynch mobs; to strike a blow against Cartesian Dualism and feel that by doing so, one has thereby struck a blow for oppressed people everywhere.

About the concept of immaterial labor

The notion of immaterial labor can be disposed of fairly quickly. In many ways it is transparently absurd.

The classic definition, by Maurizio Lazzarato is "the labor that produces the informational and cultural content of the commodity" – the 'informational content' referring to the increasing importance in production and marketing of new forms of 'cybernetics and computer control', while the second, the 'cultural content', refers to the labor of "defining and fixing cultural and artistic standards, fashions, tastes, consumer norms, and more strategically, public opinion," which, increasingly, everyone is doing all the time.[1]

---

[1] "Immaterial Labor" (http://www.generation-online.org/c/fcimmateriallabour3.htm)

On the one hand, 'immaterial workers' are "those who work in advertising, fashion, marketing, television, cybernetics, and so forth", on the other, we are all immaterial workers, insofar as we are disseminating information about brand names, creating subcultures, frequenting fan magazines or web pages or developing our own personal sense of style. As a result, production – or, at least in the sense of the production of the *value* of a commodity, what makes it something anyone would wish to buy – is no longer limited to the factory, but is dispersed across society as a whole, and becomes impossible to measure.

To some degree this is just a much more sophisticated leftist version of the rise of the service economy, etc., but there is also a very particular history, which goes back to dilemmas in Italian Workerism in the 1970s and 1980s. On the one hand, there was a stubborn Leninist assumption – promoted, for instance, by Toni Negri – that it must always be the most 'advanced' sector of the proletariat that makes up the revolutionary class. Computer and other information workers were the obvious candidates here. But the same period saw the rise of feminism and the Wages for Housework movement, which put the whole problem of unwaged, domestic labor on the political table in a way that could no longer simply be ignored. The solution was to argue that computer work and housework were really the same thing. Or, more precisely, were becoming so: since, it was argued, the increase of labor-saving devices meant that housework was becoming less and less a matter of simple drudgery, and more and more itself a matter of managing fashions, tastes and styles. The result is a genuinely strange concept, combining a kind of frenzied post-modernism, with the most clunky, old fashioned Marxist material determinism. I'll take these one at a time. Post-modern arguments, as I would define them at least, pretty much always take the same form:

> 1) begin with an extremely narrow version of what things used to be like, usually derived by taking some classic text and treating it as a precise and comprehensive treatment of reality. For instance (this is a particularly common one), assume that all capitalism up until the 1960s or 1970s worked exactly the way described in the first two or three chapters of Volume I of Marx's *Capital*
> 2) compare this to the complexities of how things actually work in the present (or even how just one thing works in the present: like a call center, a web designer, the architecture of a research lab)
> 3) declare that we can now see that lo!, sometime around 1968 or maybe 1975, the world changed completely. None of the old rules apply. Now everything is different.

The trick only works if you do not, under any circumstances, reinterpret the past in the light of the present. One could, after all, go back and ask whether it ever really made sense to think of commodities as objects whose value was simply the product of factory labor in the first place. What ever happened to all those dandies, bohemians, and flaneurs in the 19th century, not to mention newsboys, street musicians, and purveyors of patent medicines? Were they just window dressing? Actually, what about window dressing (an art famously promoted by L. Frank Baum, the creator of the *Wizard of Oz* books)? Wasn't the creation of value always in this sense a collective undertaking?

One could, even, start from the belated recognition of the importance of women's labor to re-imagine Marxist categories in general, to recognize that what we call "domestic" or even "reproductive" labor, the labor of creating people and social relations, has always been the most important form of human endeavor in *any* society, and that the creation of wheat, socks and petrochemicals always merely a means to that end, and that – what's more – most human societies have been perfectly well aware of this. One of the more peculiar features of capitalism is that it is not – that as an ideology, it encourages us to see the production of commodities as the primary business of human existence, and the mutual fashioning of human beings as somehow secondary.

Obviously all this is not to say that nothing has changed in recent years. It's not even to say that many of the connections being drawn in the immaterial labor argument are not real and important. Most of these however have been identified, and debated, in feminist literature for some time, and often to much better effect. Donna Haraway for example was already discussing the way that new communication technologies were allowing forms of 'home work' to disseminate throughout society in the 1980s. To take an obvious example: for most of the twentieth century, capitalist offices have been organized according to a gendered division of labor that mirrors the organization of upper class households: male executives engage in strategic planning while female secretaries were expected to do much of the day-to-day organizational work, along with almost all of the impression-management, communicative and interpretive labor, mostly over the phone. Gradually, these traditionally female functions have become digitized and replaced by computers; this creates a dilemma, though, because the interpretive elements of female labor (figuring out how to ensure no one's ego is bruised, that sort of thing) are precisely those that computers are *least* capable of performing. Hence, the renewed importance of what the post-Workerists like to refer to as "affective labor." This, in turn, effects how phone work is reorganized now, as globalized, but also as largely complementary to software, with interpretive work aimed more at the egos of customers than (now invisible) male bosses. The connections are all there. But it's only by starting from long-term perspectives that one can get any clear idea what's really new here, and this is precisely what the post-modern approach makes impossible.

This last example brings us to my second point, which is that very notion that there is something that can be referred to as 'immaterial labor' relies on a remarkably crude, old-fashioned kind of Marxism. Immaterial labor, we are told, is labor that produces information and culture. In other words it is 'immaterial' not because the labor itself is immaterial (how could it be?) but because it *produces* immaterial things. This idea that different sorts of labor can be sorted into more material, and less material categories according to the nature of their product is the basis for the whole conception that societies consist of a 'material base' (the production, again, of wheat, socks and petrochemicals) and 'ideological superstructure' (the production of music, culture, laws, religion, essays such as this). This is what's allowed generations of Marxists to declare that most of what we call 'culture' is really just so much fluff, at best a reflex of the really important stuff going on in fields and foundries.

What all such conceptions ignore, what is to my mind probably the single most powerful, and enduring insight of Marxist theory: that the world does not really consist (as capitalists would encourage us to believe) of a collection of discrete objects, that can then be bought and sold, but of actions and processes. This is what makes it possible for rich and powerful people to insist that what they do is somehow more abstract, more ethereal, higher and more spiritual, than everybody else. They do so by pointing at the products – poems, prayers, statutes, essays or pure abstractions like style and taste – rather than the process of making such things, which is always much messier and dirtier than the products themselves. So do such people claim to float above the muck and mire of ordinary profane existence. One would think that the first aim of a materialist approach would be to explode such pretensions – to point out, for instance, that just as the *production* of socks and silverware involves a great deal of thinking and imagining, so is the production of laws, poems and prayers an eminently material process. And indeed most contemporary materialists do, in fact, make this point. By bringing in terms like 'immaterial labor', authors like Lazzarato and Negri, bizarrely, seem to want to turn back the theory clock to somewhere around 1935.[2]

---

[2] Lazzarato, for example, argues that "the old dichotomy between 'mental and manual labor,' or between 'material labor and immaterial labor,' risks failing to grasp the new nature of productive activity, which takes the separation on board and transforms it. The split between conception and execution, between labor and creativity, between author and audience, is simultaneously transcended within the 'labor process' and reimposed as political command within the 'process of valorization'" (Maurizio Lazzarato, "General Intellect: Towards an Inquiry into Immaterial Labour", http://www.geocities.com/immateriallabour/lazzarato-immaterial-labor.html. Note here that (a) Lazzarato implies that the old manual/mental distinction was appropriate in earlier periods, and (b) what he describes appears to be for all intents and purposes exactly the kind of dialectical motion of encompassment he elsewhere condemns and rejects as a way of understanding history (or anything else): an opposition is 'transcended', yet maintained. No doubt Lazzarato

would come up with reasons about why what he is arguing is, in fact, profoundly different and un-dialectical, but for me, this is precisely the aspect of dialectics we might do well to question; a more helpful approach would be to ask how the opposition between manual and mental (etc.) is *produced.*

(As a final parenthetical note here, I suspect something very similar is happening with the notion of 'the biopolitical', the premise that it is the peculiar quality of modern states that they concern themselves with health, fertility, the regulation of life itself. The premise is extremely dubious: states have been concerned with promulgating health and fertility since the time of Frazerian sacred kings, but the same thing seems to be happening here. The insistence that we are dealing with something entirely, dramatically new becomes a way of preserving extremely old-fashioned habits of thought that might otherwise be thrown into question. After all, one of the typical ways of dismissing the importance of women's work has always been to relegate it to the domain of nature. The process of caring for, educating, nurturing and generally crafting human beings is reduced to the implicitly biological domain of 'reproduction', which is then considered secondary for that very reason. Instead of using new developments to problematize this split, the impulse seems to be to declare that just as commodity production has exploded the factory walls and come to pervade every aspect of our experience, so has biological reproduction exploded the walls of the home and pervaded everything as well – this time, through the state. The result is a kind of sledge-hammer approach that once again, makes it almost impossible to reexamine our original theoretical assumptions.)

The art world as a form of politics

This reluctance to question old-fashioned theoretical assumptions has real consequences on the resulting analysis. Consider Negri's contribution to the conference. He begins by arguing that each change in the development of the productive forces since the 1840s corresponds to a change in the dominant style of high art: the realism of the period 1848-1870 corresponds to one of the concentration of industry and the working class, impressionism, from 1871-1914, marks the period of the 'professional worker', that sees the world to be dissolved and reconstructed, after 1917, abstract art reflects the new abstraction of labor-power with the introduction of scientific management, and so on. The changes in the material infrastructure – of industry – are thus reflected in the ideological superstructure. The resulting analysis is revealing, no doubt, even fun if one is into that sort of thing, but it sidesteps the obvious fact that the production of art is an industry, and one connected to capital, marketing and design in any number of (historically shifting) ways. One need not ask who is buying these things, who is funding the institutions, where artists live, how else are their techniques being employed. By defining art as belonging to the immaterial domain, its materialities, or even its entanglement in other abstractions (like money) need not be addressed.

This is perhaps not the place for a prolonged analysis, but a few notes on what's called 'the art world' might seem to be in order. It is a common perception, not untrue, that at least since the 1920s, the art world has been in a kind of permanent institutionalized crisis. One could even say that what we call 'the art world' has become the ongoing management of this crisis. The crisis, of course, is about the nature of art. The entire apparatus of the art world – critics, journals, curators, gallery owners, dealers, flashy magazines and the people who leaf through them and argue about them in factories-turned-chichi-cafes in gentrifying neighborhoods... – could be said to exist to come up with an answer to one single question: what is art? Or, to be more precise, to come up with some answer other than the obvious one, which is 'whatever we can convince very rich people to buy.'

I am really not trying to be cynical. Actually, I think the dilemma to some degree, flows from the very nature of politics. One thing the explosion of the avant garde did accomplish was to destroy the boundaries between art and politics, to make clear in fact that art was always, really, a form of politics (or at least that this was always one thing that it was). As a result, the art world has been faced with the same fundamental dilemma as any form of politics: the impossibility of establishing its own legitimacy.

Let me explain what I mean by this.
It is the peculiar feature of political life that within it, behavior that could only otherwise be considered insane is perfectly effective. If you managed to convince everyone on earth that you can breathe under water, it won't make any difference: if you try it, you will still drown. On the other hand, if you could convince everyone in the entire world that you were the King of France, then you would actually be the King of France. (In fact, it would probably work just to convince a substantial portion of the French civil service and military.)

This is the essence of politics. Politics is that dimension of social life in which things really do become true if enough people believe them. The problem is that in order to play the game effectively, one can never acknowledge its essence. No king would openly admit he is king just because people think he is. Political power has to be constantly recreated by persuading others to recognize one's power; to do so, one pretty much invariably has to convince them that one's power has some basis other than their recognition. That basis may be almost anything— divine grace, character, genealogy, national destiny. But "make me your leader, because if you do, I will be your leader" is not in itself a particularly compelling argument.

In this sense, politics is very similar to magic, which in most times and places – as I discovered in Madagascar – is simultaneously recognized as something that works, because people believe that it works; but also, that only works, because people do not believe it works only because people believe it works. For this is why magic, whether in ancient Thessaly or the contemporary Trobriand Islands, always seems to dwell in an uncertain territory somewhere between poetic expression and outright fraud. And of course, the same can usually be said of politics.

If so, for the art world to recognize itself as a form of politics is also to recognize itself as something both magical, and a confidence game – a kind of scam.

Such then is the nature of the permanent crisis. In political economy terms, of course, the art world has become largely an appendage to finance capital. This is not to say that it takes on the nature of finance capital (in many ways, in its forms, values and practices, is almost exactly the opposite) – but it is to say it follows it around, its galleries and studios clustering and proliferating around the fringes of the neighborhoods where financiers live and work in global cities everywhere, from New York and London, to Basel and Miami.

Contemporary art holds out a special appeal to financiers, I suspect, because it allows for a kind of short circuit in the normal process of value creation. It is a world where the mediations that normally intervene between the proletarian world of material production and the airy heights of fictive capital are, essentially, yanked away.

Ordinarily, it is the working class world in which people make themselves intimately familiar with the uses of welding gear, glue, dyes and sheets of plastic, power saws, thread, cement, and toxic industrial solvents. It is among the upper class, or at last upper middle class world where even economics turns into politics: where everything is impression management and things really can become true because you say so. Between these two worlds lie endless tiers of mediation. Factories and workshops in China and Southeast Asia produce clothing designed by companies in New York, paid for with capital invested on the basis of calculations of debt, interest, anticipation of future demand and market fluctuations in Bahrain, Tokyo and Zurich, repackaged in turn into an endless variety of derivatives – futures, options, various traded and arbitraged and repackaged again onto even greater levels of mathematical abstraction to the point where the very idea of trying to establish a relation with any physical product, goods or services, is simply inconceivable. Yet the same bankers and traders who produce these complex financial instruments also like to surround themselves with artists, people who are always busy making things – a kind of imaginary proletariat assembled by finance capital, producing unique products out of for the most part very inexpensive materials, objects said financiers can baptize, consecrate, through money and thus turn into art, thus displaying its ability to transform the basest of materials into objects worth far, far more than gold.

It is never clear, in this context, who exactly is scamming whom.[3] Everyone – artists, dealers, critics, collectors alike – continue to pay lip service on the old 19th century Romantic conception that the value of a work of art emerges directly from the unique genius of some individual artist. But none of them really believe that's all, or even most, of what's actually going on. Many artists are deeply cynical about what they do. But even those who are the most idealistic can only feel they are pulling something off when they are able to create enclaves, however small, where they can experiment with forms of life, exchange, and production which are – if not downright communistic (which they often are), then at any rate, about as far from the forms ordinarily promoted by capital anyone can get to experience in a large urban center – and to get capitalists to pay for it, directly or indirectly. Critics and dealers are aware, if often slightly uneasy with the fact that, the value of an artwork is to some degree their own creation; collectors, in turn, seem much less uneasy with the knowledge that in the end, it is their money that makes an object into art. Everyone is willing to play around with the dilemma, to incorporate it into the nature of art itself. I have a friend, a sculptor, who once made a sculpture consisting simply of the words "I NEED MONEY', and then tried to sell it to collectors to pay the rent. It was snapped up instantly. Are the collectors who snap up this sort of thing suckers, or are they reveling in their own ability to play Marcel Duchamp?

Duchamp, after all, justified his famous 'fountain', his attempt to buy an ordinary urinal and place it in an art show, by saying that while he might not have made or modified the object, he had 'chosen' it, and thus transformed it as a concept. I suspect the full implications of this act only dawned on him later. If so, it would help explain why he eventually abandoned participating in the art world entirely and spent the last forty years of his life claiming he was simply playing chess, one of the few activities that, he occasionally pointed out, could not possibly be commoditized.

---

[3] That is, within the art world. The fact that increasing numbers of these complex financial instruments are themselves being revealed to be little more than scams adds what can only be described as an additional kink.

Perhaps the problem runs even deeper. Perhaps this is simply the kind of dilemma that necessarily ensues when two incommensurable systems of value face off against each other. The original, romantic conception of the artist – and hence, the very idea of art in the modern sense – arose around the time of industrial revolution. Probably this is no coincidence. As Godbout and Caille have pointed out, there is a certain complementarity. Industrialism was all about the mass production of physical objects, but the producers themselves were invisible, anonymous – about them one knew nothing. Art was about the production of unique physical objects, and their value was seen as emerging directly from the equally unique genius of their individual producers – about whom one knew everything. Even more, the production of commodities was seen as a purely economic activity. One produced fishcakes or aluminum siding, in order to make money. The production of art was not seen as an essentially economic activity. Like the pursuit of scientific knowledge, or spiritual grace, or the love of family for that matter, the love of art has always been seen as expressing a fundamentally different, higher form of value. Genuine artists do not produce art simply in order to make money. But unlike astronomers, priests, or housewives, they do have to sell their products on the market in order to survive. What's more, the market value of their work is dependent on the perception that it was produced in the pursuit of something other than market value. People argue endlessly about what that 'something other' is – beauty, inspiration, virtuosity, aesthetic form – I would myself argue that nowadays, at least, it is impossible to say it is just one thing, rather, art has become a field for play and experiment with the very idea of value – but all pretty much agree that, were an artist to be seen as simply in it for the money, his work would be worth less of it.

I suspect this is a dilemma anyone might face, when trying to maintain some kind of space of autonomy in the face of the market. Those pursuing other forms of value can attempt to insulate themselves from the market. They can come to some sort of accommodation or even symbiosis. Or they can end up in a situation where each side sees itself as ripping the other off.

What I really want to emphasize though is that none of this means that any of these spaces are any less real. We have a tendency to assume that, since capital and its attendant forms of value are so clearly dominant, then everything that happens in the world somehow partakes of its essence. We assume capitalism forms a total system, and that the only real significance of any apparent alternative is the role it plays in reproducing it. Myself, I feel this logic is deeply flawed – even disastrous. For two hundred years at least, artists and those drawn to them have created enclaves where it has been possible to experiment with forms of work, exchange and production radically different from those promoted by capital. While they are not always self-consciously revolutionary, artistic circles have had a persistent tendency to overlap with revolutionary circles; presumably, precisely because these have been spaces where people can experiment with radically different, less alienated forms of life. The fact that all this is made possible by money percolating downwards from finance capital does not make such spaces 'ultimately' a product of capitalism any more than the fact a privately owned factory uses state-supplied and regulated utilities and postal services, relies on police to protect its property and courts to enforce its contracts, makes the cars they turn out 'ultimately' products of socialism. Total systems don't really exist, they're just stories we tell ourselves, and the fact that capital is dominant now does not mean that it will always be.

On prophecy and social theory

Now, this is hardly a detailed analysis of value formation in the art world. It is only the crudest preliminary sketch. But it's already a thousand times more concrete than anything yet produced by theorists of immaterial labor.

Granted, Continental theory has a notorious tendency to float above the surface of things, only rarely touching down in empirical reality. Lazzarato has a particularly annoying habit of claiming his concepts emerge from a large body of recent 'empirical research', which he never, however, actually cites or specifically refers to. Negri tends to throw everything, all the specific gestures, exchanges, and transformations into a kind of giant blender called 'real subsumption' – whereby since everything is labor, and all forms of labor operate under the logic of capital, there's rarely much need to parse the differences between one form and another (let alone analyze the actual organization of, say, a collections agency, or the fashion industry, or any particular capitalist supply chain).

But in another sense this criticism is unfair. It assumes that Negri and Lazzarato are to be judged as social theorists, in the sense that their work is meant primarily to develop concepts that can be useful in understanding the current state of capitalism or the forms of resistance ranged against it – or at any rate that it can be judged primarily on the degree to which it can. Certainly, any number of young scholars have been trying to adopt these concepts to such purposes, with rather mixed results. But I don't think this was ever their primary aim. They are first and foremost prophets.

Prophecy, of course, existed long before social theory proper, and in many ways anticipated it. In the Abrahamic tradition, that runs from

Judaism through Christianity to Islam, prophets are not simply people who speak of future events. They are people who provide revelation of hidden truths about the world, which may include knowledge of events yet to come, to pass, but need not necessarily. One could argue that revolutionary thought, and critical social theory, both have their origins in prophecy. At the same time, prophecy is clearly a form of politics. This is not only because prophets were invariably concerned with social justice. It is because they created social movements, even, new societies: as Spinoza emphasized, it was the prophets who effectively produced the Hebrew people, by creating a framework for their history. Negri has always been quite up front about his own desire to play a similar role for what he likes to call 'the Multitude'. He is less interested in describing realities than in bringing them into being. A political discourse, he says, should "aspire to fulfill a Spinozist prophetic function, the function of an immanent desire that organizes the Multitude."[4] The same could be said of theories of immaterial labor. They're not really descriptive. For its most ardent proponents, immaterial labor is really important because it's seen to represent a new form of communism: ways of creating value by forms of social cooperation so dispersed that just about everyone could be said to take part, much as they do in the collective creation of language, and in a way that makes it impossible to calculate inputs and outputs, where there is no possibility of accounting. Capitalism, which is reduced increasingly to simply realizing the value created by such communistic practices, is thereby reduced to a purely parasitical force, a kind of feudal overlord extracting rent from forms of creativity entirely alien to it. We are already living under communism, if only we come to realize it. This is, of course, the real role of the prophet: to organize the desires of the Multitude, to help these already-existing forms of communism burst out of their increasingly artificial shackles. Beside this epochal task, the concrete analysis of the organization of real-life TV studios or cell phone dealerships seems petty and irrelevant.

In contrast, the main body of social theory as we know it today does not trace back to such performative revolutionary gestures, but precisely from their failure. Sociology sprang from the ruins of the French revolution; Marx's *Capital* was written to try to understand the failure of the revolutions of 1848, just as most contemporary French theory emerged from reflections on what went wrong in May '68. Social theory aims to understand social realities; social reality in turn is, first and foremost, that which resists attempts to simply call prophet visions into existence or even (perhaps especially) to impose them through the apparatus of the state. Since all good social theory does also contain an element of prophecy, the result is a constant internal tension; in its own way as profound as the tension I earlier suggested lay at the heart of politics. But the work of Negri and his associates clearly leans very heavily on the prophetic side of the equation.

Concerning the fullness of time

At this point I think I can return to my initial question: why does one need a revolutionary philosopher to help us think about art? Why does one call in a prophet?

The answer would appear to be: One calls in a prophet, because prophets above all, know how to speak compellingly about their audience's place in history.

Certainly this is the role in which Negri, Bifo and the rest have now been cast. They have become impresarios of the historical moment. When their ideas are invoked by artists or philosophers, this is largely what those artists and philosophers seem to be looking for. When they are brought on stage at public events, this is mainly what is expected of them. Their job is to explain why the time we live in is unique, why the processes we see crystallizing around us are unprecedented; different in quality, different in kind, from anything that has ever come before.

Certainly, this is what each one of the four, in their own way, actually did. They might not have had much to say about specific works of art or specific forms of labor, but each provided a detailed assessment of where we stood in history. For Lazzarato, the significant thing was that we had moved from a society of discipline to one of security; for Revel, what was really important was the move from formal to real subsumption of labor under capital. For Bifo, we had moved from an age of connection to one of conjunction; for Negri, the new stage of Contemporaneity that had replaced post-modernism. Each dutifully explained how we had entered into a new age, and described some of its qualities and implications, along with an assessment of its potential for some sort of radical political transformation.

It's easy to see why the art world would provide a particularly eager market for this sort of thing. Art has become a world where – as Walter Benjamin once said of fashion – everything is always new, but nothing ever changes. In the world of fashion, of course, it's possible to generate a sense of novelty simply by playing around with color, patterns, styles and hemlines. The visual arts, though, do not have such a luxury. They have always seen themselves as entangled in a larger world of culture and politics, that they are not simply playing around with form. Hence, the permanent need to conjure up a sense that we are in a profoundly new historical moment, even if art theorists attempting such an act of conjuration often seem to find themselves with less and less to work with.

---

[4] *Empire*, p. 66.

There is another reason, I think, why revolutionary thinkers are particularly well-suited to such a task. One can come to understand it, I think, by examining what would otherwise seem to be a profound contradiction in the all of the speakers' approaches to history. In each case, we are presented with a series of historical stages: from societies of discipline to societies of security, from conjunction to connection, etc. We are not dealing with a series of complete conceptual breaks; at least, no one seems to imagine that it is impossible to understand any one stage from the perspective of any of the others. But oddly, all of the speakers in question subscribed to the theory that history *should* be conceived as a series of complete conceptual breaks, so total, in fact, that it's hard to see how this would be possible. In part, this is the legacy of Marxism, which always tends to insist that since capitalism forms an all-encompassing totality that shapes our most basic assumptions about the nature of society, we simply cannot conceive what a future society would be like. (Though no Marxist, oddly, seems to think we should have similar problems trying to understand past societies.) In this case, though, it is just as much the legacy of Michel Foucault,[5] who radicalized this idea of a series of all-encompassing historical stages even further with his notion of epistemes: that the very conception of truth changes completely from one historical period to the next. Here, too, each historical period forms such a total system that it is impossible to imagine one gradually transforming into another; instead, we have a series of conceptual revolutions, of total breaks or ruptures.

All of the speakers at the conference were drawing, in one way or another, on both the Marxian and Foucauldian traditions – and some of the terms used for historical stages ('real subsumption', 'societies of discipline'…) drew explicitly on one or the other. Thus, all of them were faced with the same conceptual problem. How could it be possible to come up with such a typology? How is it possible for someone trapped inside one historical period to be able to grasp the overall structure of history through which one stage replaces the other?

The prophet, of course, has an answer to this question. Just as we can only grasp an individual's life as a story once he is dead, it is only from the perspective of the end of time that we can grasp the story of history. It doesn't matter that we do not really know what the messianic Future will be like: it can serve as the Archimedean point, the time outside time about which we can know nothing that nonetheless makes knowledge possible.

---

[5] Really, I would say, it is the legacy of structuralism. Foucault is remembered mainly as a post-structuralist, but he began as an arch-structuralist, and this aspect of his philosophy in no sense changed over the course of his career but if anything grew stronger.

Of course, Bifo was explicitly arguing that the Future itself is dead. The twentieth century, he insisted, had been the 'century of the future' (that's why he began his analysis with the Futurists). But we have left that now, and moved on to a century with no future, only precarity. We have come to a point where it is impossible to even imagine projecting ourselves forwards in time in any meaningful way, where the only radical gesture left to us is, therefore, self-mutilation or suicide. Certainly, this reflected a certain prevailing mood in radical circles. We really do lack a sense of where we stand in history. And it runs well beyond radical circles: the North Atlantic world has fallen into a somewhat apocalyptic mood of late. Everyone is brooding on great catastrophes, peak oil, economic collapse, ecological devastation. But I would argue that even outside revolutionary circles, the Future in its old-fashioned, revolutionary sense, can never really go away. Our world would make no sense without it.

So we are faced with a dilemma. The revolutionary Future appears increasingly implausible to most of us, but neither can we simply get rid of it. As a result, it begins to collapse into the present. Hence, for instance, the insistence that communism is already here, if only we knew how to see it. The Future has become a kind of hidden dimension of reality, an immanent presence lying behind the mundane surface of the world, with a constant potential to break out, but only in tiny, imperfect flashes. In this sense, we are forced to live with two very different futures: that which we suspect will actually come to pass – perhaps humdrum, perhaps catastrophic, certainly not in any sense redemptive – and The Future in the old revolutionary, apocalyptic sense of the term: the fulfillment of time, the unraveling of contradictions. Genuine knowledge of this Future is impossible, but it is only from the perspective of this unknowable Outside that any real knowledge of the present is possible. The Future has become our Dreamtime.

One could see it as something like St. Augustine's conception of Eternity, the ground that unifies Past, Present and Future, because it precedes the creation of Time. But I think the notion of the Dreamtime is, if anything, even more appropriate. Aboriginal Australian societies could only make sense of themselves in relation to a distant past that worked utterly differently (in which, for instance animals could become humans and back again), a past which was at once irretrievable, but always somehow there, and into which humans could transport ourselves in dreams and trances so as to attain true knowledge. As with their Past, so now with our Future. It is a myth, but a myth constantly elaborated, as in our endless habit of watching science fiction fantasies on TV and in the movies, even though we no longer believe, as we once did, that the future is really likely to be like that. In this sense, the speakers at our conference found themselves cast in the role not even of prophets, perhaps, but of shamans, technicians of the sacred, capable of moving back and forth between cosmic dimensions – and of course, like any magician, both a sort of artist in their own right and at the same time a sort of trickster and a fraud.

Not surprising, then, that as the sincere revolutionaries they were, most seemed to find themselves slightly puzzled by how they had arrived here.

A final note

Perhaps this seems unduly harsh. I have, after all, trashed the very notion of immaterial labor, accused post-Workerists (or at least the strain represented at this conference) of using flashy, superficial post-modern arguments to disguise a clunky antiquated version of Marxism, and suggested they are engaged in an essentially theological exercise, which while it might be helpful for those interested in playing games of artistic fashion or imagining broad historical vistas, provides almost nothing in the way of useful tools for concrete social analysis of the art world or anything else. I think that everything I said was true. But I don't want to leave the reader with the impression that there is nothing of value here.

First of all, I actually do agree that thinkers like these are useful in helping us conceptualize the historical moment. And not only in the prophetic-political-magical sense of offering descriptions that aim to bring new realities into being. I find the idea of a revolutionary future that is already with us, the notion that in a sense we already live in communism, in its own way quite compelling. The problem is, being prophets, they always have to frame their arguments in apocalyptic terms. Would it not be better to, as I suggested earlier, reexamine the past in the light of the present? Perhaps communism has always been with us. We are just trained not to see it. Perhaps everyday forms of communism are really – as Kropotkin in his own way suggested in *Mutual Aid*, even though even he was never willing to realize the full implications of what he was saying – the basis for most significant forms of human achievement, even those ordinarily attributed to capitalism. If we can extricate ourselves from the shackles of fashion, the need to constantly say that whatever is happening now is necessarily unique and unprecedented (and thus, in a sense, unchanging, since everything apparently must always be this way) we might be able to grasp history as a field of permanent possibility, in which there is no particular reason we can't at least try to begin building a redemptive future at any time. There have been artists trying to contribute to doing so, in small ways, since time immemorial – some, as part of bona fide social movements. It's not clear that social theorists – good ones anyway – are doing anything all so entirely different.

Previously published in: *The Commoner*, April 2008; also availabe at: http://www.commoner.org.uk/?p=33

Glossary

Academic managerialism: the method of running higher education according to commercial values and rules; combines with peer review to outflank resistance to new forms of controlling academic labour; reinforces disciplinary boundaries through centralised systems of bureaucratic standardisation and control.

Adjustable/Variable rate mortgages: (or floating rate mortgage) a mortgage loan where the interest rate varies to reflect market conditions. The interest rate will normally vary with changes to the base rate of the central bank and reflects changing costs on credit markets. This method of variation benefits lenders by ensuring profit, which it does by passing the interest rate risk to the borrower/home owner.

Bulimia-learning: a fundamental illness in contemporary higher education, found particularly among bachelor students who are forced, in the shortest time possible, to stuff as much knowledge into themselves as possible, to throw it up shortly afterwards, and finally forget it for all time.

Commonification: war on commodification, the move from commodity to common. The process of transforming that which has been privatised, commodified or enclosed into commons.

Credit bubble: an economic bubble (sometimes referred to as a speculative bubble, a market bubble, a price bubble, a financial bubble, or speculative mania) is trade in high volumes at prices that vary considerably to actual or intrinsic values.

De-skilling: 1. to eliminate the need for skilled labor in (an industry), especially by the introduction of high technology. 2. to downgrade (a job or occupation) from a skilled to a semi-skilled or unskilled position.

Economic growth: "As we strengthen our military to meet the challenges of the 21st century, we must also work together to achieve important goals for the American people here at home. This work begins with keeping our economy growing... and I encourage you all to go shopping more."[1]

End-of-the-world trade: the purchase of insurance against the failure of the modern capitalist system.[2]

Export Processing Zones (EPZ): areas with extremely favourable tax regimes for business, slack environmental regulations, and anti-union laws, in a context of widespread poverty and increased dependence on the market, all helping industries that want to escape higher wages and stronger regulations.

Fictitious capital: money that is thrown into circulation as capital without any material basis in commodities or productive activity.[3]

Grading system: a means for the production of social class as well as subjugation to the rules of the labour market and the political economy.

Greater fool theory: portrays economic bubbles as driven by the behaviour of perennially optimistic market participants (the fools) who buy overvalued assets in anticipation of selling it to other rapacious speculators (the greater fools) at a much higher price. The bubbles continue as long as the fools can find greater fools to pay up for the overvalued asset. The bubbles will only end when the greater fool becomes the greatest fool who pays the top price for the overvalued asset, and can no longer find another buyer to pay for it at a higher price.

How to make a living as a visual artist: what the artist receives is determined by the production market, and the production market is determined by the exchange market, and the exchange market is subject to its own self-interests, to the whims and greed of the private, the corporate and state powers involved in art investment.[4]

Hypocriticality: anti-capitalist critique that is sponsored by banks.

Intensity of labour: means increased expenditure of labour in a given time. Hence a working-day of more intense labour is embodied in more products than is one of less intense labour, the length of each day being the same. Increased productiveness of labour also, it is true, will supply more products in a given working-day. But in this latter case, the value of each single product falls, for it costs less labour than before; in the former case, that value remains unchanged, for each article costs the same labour as before. Here we have an increase in the number of products, unaccompanied by a fall in their individual prices: as their number increases, so does the sum of their prices.[5]

Ivy League, The: an athletic conference comprising eight private institutions of higher education located in the Northeastern United States. The term is most commonly used to refer to those eight schools considered as a group. The term also has connotations of academic excellence, selectivity in admissions, and a reputation for social elitism.

Lifelong learning: lifelong subservience to the education industry, in terms of needing to pay for new skills, with wages that are decreasing, to get new jobs that will be de-skilled again in the future, thus precipitating more expensive learning in order to remain in the employment market.

Line manager squeeze: setting the line manager an impossible task – e.g. sacrificing quality of service and staff break times in order to sell more merchandise. The longer-term effect is to damage the brand and reputation of the company – the executive management will have retired by then, but line managers will still be trying to pay off their mortgage doing the same old job.

Linguistic commonification: the reclamation/making common of the definition of words, such as, for example, 'common' or 'autonomy'.

Market value: viewed from the standpoint of the objective relations of capitalist society, the greatest work of art is equal to a certain quantity of manure.[6]

Meritocracy: 1. a system in which the talented are chosen and moved ahead on the basis of their achievement. 2. leadership selected on the basis of intellectual criteria.

Mortgage: the grip of death (Latin).

Non-capitalist life: the elements of our lives that we are already living, and those still to be developed that are outside, resistant to, and not co-opted by capitalism.

Online learning: you can save a tremendous amount of money when you're piping courses and programmes into somebody's living room and you don't have to pay for buildings, you don't have to pay staff to teach, you know a few teachers and a few electronic programmes will be enough to reach a large number of people with substantial monetary results. Very often soldiers are recruited with the incentive that they will receive a degree if they join the army. So online education is very good, because you can be deployed in a far off country, maybe even in Iraq, and at the same time get your B.A.[7]

PAYE: the Pay As You Earn system is a method of paying income tax. The taxpayer's employer deducts tax from the wages or occupational pension before paying the wages. Wages include sick pay and maternity pay.

Primitive accumulation: when Western capital sucks Third World labour power, whose costs of reproduction it did not pay for, into the world division of labour, whether in Indonesia or in Los Angeles, that's primitive accumulation. When capital loots the natural environment and does not pay the replacement costs for that damage, that's primitive accumulation. When capital runs capital plant and infrastructure into the ground (the story of much of the U.S. and the U.K. economies since the 1960s) that's primitive accumulation. When capital pays workers non-reproductive wages, (wages too low to produce a new generation of workers) that's primitive accumulation, too.[8]

Privatised profit – socialised risk: profit is made the property of banks, hedge funds, private equity, etc. while the risk involved for making those profits falls on the taxpayer (e.g. when governments bail out failing banks) and on society in general (e.g. when jobs are lost or pension funds destroyed through the insane speculations made by banks).

Repetitive Strain Injury (RSI): any of a loose group of conditions resulting from overuse of a tool, e.g. computer, guitar or knife, or other activity that requires repeated movements. The medically accepted condition in which it occurs is when muscles in these areas are kept tense for very long periods of time, due to poor posture and/or repetitive motions.

Securitization: the process of taking an illiquid asset, or group of assets, and through financial engineering, transforming them into a security.

Structural Adjustment Program (SAP): devalue the currency, thus making imports more expensive and enforcing a cut in real wages; privatise water, education, healthcare and other national resources, thus opening them up to restructuring, hence unemployment, cut social spending; cut subsidies on necessities like food and fuel; open up markets to foreign investors; promote competitive exports, which will help to repay the debt.[9]

Text: like any particular piece of textile, is open-ended and its materials can be both extended, as well as used in the creation of other texts.[10]

Footnotes:

[1] George W. Bush, Predictions for 2007

[2] Donald MacKenzie, "End-of-the-world trade", May 2008, http://www.lrb.co.uk/v30/n09/mack01_.html

[3] David Harvey, *Limits to Capital*, (2006).

[4] Ian Burn, "Pricing Works of Art", *The Fox* #1, 1975.

[5] Karl Marx, *Capital*, Volume 1, Chapter 17, Section 2 http://www.marxists.org/archive/marx/work s/1867-c1/ch17.htm#S1

[6] Ian Burn, "Pricing Works of Art", *The Fox* #1, 1975, Marx

[7] Silvia Federici, "Education and the Enclosure of Knowledge in the Global University", A Talk at the School of Geography, University of Leeds.

[8] Loren Goldner, "Fictitious Capital for Beginners", http://home.earthlink.net/~lrgoldner/imperi alism.html

[9] Massimo De Angelis, "Next Lap in the Rat Race? From Sub-Prime Crisis to the "Impasse" of Global Capital", republished in this journal.

[10] George Caffentzis. "A Critique of Commodified Education and Knowledge", posted on *The Commoner*, April 25 2008. http://www.commoner.org.uk/?p=35

Contributors

Massimo De Angelis is Professor of Political Economy at the University of East London. Working in the broad tradition of Autonomist Marxism, his most recent book is *The Beginning of History: Global Capital and Value Struggles* (Pluto Press: 2007). He is editor of the web-journal *The Commoner* (http://www.commoner.org.uk/). M.Deangelis@uel.ac.uk

John Barker has been involved with a wide range of anti-capitalist, organised labour struggles since the late 1960s. His essays on political, social and cultural issues have also been published in *Variant* and *Mute* magazines. His memoir *Bending the Bars: Prison Stories of an Angry Brigade Member* was published by Christie books in 2006. harrier@easynet.co.uk

Marc Bousquet is the founding editor of *Workplace: A Journal for Academic Labour* (www.workplace-gsc.com) and author of the book *How the University Works: Higher Education and the Low-Wage Nation*.

Chto delat?/What is to be done? was founded in early 2003 in Petersburg by a workgroup of artists, critics, philosophers and writers from Petersburg, Moscow and Nizhny Novgorod with the goal of merging political theory, art and activism. Since then, Chto delat has been publishing an English-Russian newspaper on issues central to engaged culture, with a special focus on the relationship between a repoliticization of Russian intellectual culture and its broader international context. www.chtodelat.org

Silvia Federici is a scholar, teacher and activist from the radical Feminist Marxist tradition and Professor Emerita at Hofstra University. She co-founded the International Feminist Collective (1972), launching the international campaign for "wages for housework" in the U.S. and the Committee for Academic Freedom in Africa (1991). Her book *Caliban and the Witch: Women, the Body and Primitive Accumulation* was published in 2004. nucszf@hofstra.edu

Rebecca Gordon Nesbitt has worked for more than a decade in the field of visual art. She undertook an MRes in Social Research at the University of Strathclyde, for which she continued her research into the privatisation of culture and the role of contemporary art in challenging the status quo. Her PhD, looking at cultural policy in post-revolutionary Cuba, seeks to examine how critical practice can be encouraged, or stifled, by cultural policy. Examples of her fact and fiction may be found at: www.shiftyparadigms.org. rebecca.gordon-nesbitt@strath.ac.uk

David Graeber is an American anthropologist, currently employed at Goldsmiths, University of London. He is the author of *Lost People, Toward an Anthropological Theory of Value, Possibilities, and Fragments of an Anarchist Anthropology* along with a forthcoming ethnography of direct action, and has been involved in such groups as the Direct Action Network, People's Global Action, and the Industrial Workers of the World. d.graeber@gold.ac.uk

Stewart Martin is a member of the editorial collective and reviews editor of the journal *Radical Philosophy,* and teaches philosophy and art at Middlesex University. S.C.Martin@mdx.ac.uk

PECAN, the Private Equity Creative Action Network is a growing network of labour, environmental and cultural organisers from England, Italy, Germany, France and the United States who have been exploring issues of precarity, debt and the emerging crisis of food, fuel and finances. This network has been evolving over the past two years, organising solidarity actions with labour struggles. privateequitysucks@googlemail.com

MeineAkademie was founded as a political and artistic collective on the occasion of the opening of the Volkswagen university library of the Technical University and the University of the Arts in Berlin in December 2004. Organising campaigns to inform the public and holding seminars, the group researched the political and economical background that led to the public-private partnership between the universities and Volkswagen. ***Johannes Raether*** was a member of this group. He is an artist living in Berlin. www.meineakademie.tk; meineakademie@gmx.net

Tiziana Terranova has published her research on technological subcultures and science in Italian and English in journals such as *New Formations, Science and Culture, Derive e Approdi* and the online journal *The Difference Engine.* She is author of "Corpi nella Rete" ("Bodies in the Net"), 1996, and "Network Culture – Politics for the Information Age", 2004.

Joen P-Vedel: lives and studies art in Copenhagen, he is currently helping his father repair an old roof, it leaks.

Many thanks to all the contributors

This publication is self-sponsored.
Rosa Kerosene, October 2008.
Collective work, that's it.

rosakerosene@gmail.com